At Issue

Troll Factories:
Russia's Web Brigades

Other Books in the At Issue Series

At Issue

| Troll Factories:
| Russia's Web Brigades

Andrew Karpan, Book Editor

GREENHAVEN
PUBLISHING

Published in 2019 by Greenhaven Publishing, LLC
353 3rd Avenue, Suite 255, New York, NY 10010

Articles in Greenhaven Publishing anthologies are often edited for length to meet page
requirements. In addition, original titles of these works are changed to clearly present
the main thesis and to explicitly indicate the author's opinion. Every effort is made to
ensure that Greenhaven Publishing accurately reflects the original intent of the authors.
Every effort has been made to trace the owners of the copyrighted material.

Cover image: Gorodenkoff/Shutterstock.com

Library of Congress Cataloging-in-Publication Data

Names: Karpan, Andrew, editor.
Title: Troll factories : Russia's web brigades / Andrew Karpan, book editor.
Description: New York : Greenhaven Publishing, [2019] | Series: At issue | Audience:
  Grade 9 to 12. | Includes bibliographical references and index.
Identifiers: LCCN 2018024893| ISBN 9781534503830 (library bound) | ISBN
  9781534504530 (pbk.)
Subjects: LCSH: Computer security—Russia (Federation) | Cyberspace—Political aspects
  —Russia (Federation) | Hacking—Russia (Federation)
Classification: LCC QA76.9.A25 T76 2018 | DDC 303.48/2—dc23
LC record available at https://lccn.loc.gov/2018024893

Manufactured in the United States of America

Website: http://greenhavenpublishing.com

Contents

Introduction

The 2016 presidential election will go down in history as the first to be primarily negotiated over social media, its winner better known for his popularly pugnacious Twitter account than the lifetimes of government or military work that marked his forty-four predecessors. But while voting booths preclude anyone without US citizenship from entering, no such requirement exists for users of social media platforms: an often-anonymous sea of millions of profiles, a public forum where anyone can enter. The concept is freeing—at no other time in human history have so many voices been able to express themselves without fear of official reprimand. But almost as soon as that freedom presented itself, it was discovered that many of those voices were not actually real. The same governments that had, in the past, thrown journalists in jail and printed propaganda pamphlets to replace them were now generating fictional supporters with the click of a button, bypassing the democratic concept of majoritarian discourse by simply inventing majorities. The 2016 presidential election became the first in our history to be negotiated by internet trolls—people who intentionally stir controversy and start arguments on social media to manipulate public opinion or create chaos.

Many of these trolls, we found out, happened to be based in a nondescript office building in a fashionable neighborhood slightly north of St. Petersburg, Russia. Vladimir Putin, Russia's president, had taken office in 2000, shortly after the internet became accessible to millions around the world. At that time, the primary social networks still consisted of message boards, and debate was largely limited to website comment sections. However, as one observer had noticed a few years later, "the commentaries of average Russians are striking in the ferocious unanimity of their readers."[1] Journalists began suspecting, for the first time, that the internet was being occupied by people who weren't "real" but were, instead, fake names meant to camouflage the fact that the same comments were being paid for and made over and over again. "Who posts at night on someone else's LJ? [LiveJournal]" asked a headline in *New Region*, a Russian news agency that later shut down after its editor-in-chief was found dead. By no means was this only happening in Russia—the use of false or misleading identities on the internet were called "sock puppets" in early Usenet circles in the late 1990s.[2] But something already felt officious and organized about these early, shadowy commenters, and many Russian journalists soon came upon the word бригадники (*brigadniki*). The web brigades.

Many suspected this was the work of the Federal Security Service (FSB), the government police force that eventually succeeded the infamous KGB after the collapse of the Soviet Union. Before being elected President, Putin had also served as director of the FSB and after his election, he placed the FSB under the President's direct control. Many of the ferociously unanimous online opinions were congruent to positions the Putin administration had taken. But confirming these suspicions and even conducting research on the topic was difficult. Jessikka Aro, a Finnish journalist, ended up subject to a campaign of seemingly coordinated online abuse after she issued a call to her audience to speak out about their experiences dealing with what she called Russia's "troll army" on the internet. "Everything in my life went to hell thanks to the trolls," she told the *New York Times* in 2016.[3]

Confirmation that Putin-affiliated institutions were part of a large-scale trolling operation came when leaked emails showed that a Russian youth group called Nashi, whose work Putin often visibly supported, had been paying bloggers to leave hundreds of comments on news articles that were critical of Putin. Later, a St. Petersburg-based company called the Internet Research Agency (IRA)—funded by the Russian businessman Yevgeny Prigozhin, whose catering company personally served Putin events—was discovered to be paying bloggers full-time to advance Putin talking points on platforms like Twitter, Facebook, and VKontakte, a

Russian social network website. By then, the interests of Putin and the FSB had turned away from Russian domestic politics. Russian trolling operations were suspected of involvement in the media cycle surrounding the 2016 Brexit vote in the UK, a political situation that Putin—a vocal opponent of the EU—was thought to be invested in. Later that year, after the US presidential election, the Obama administration made official its suspicion that the FSB, in collaboration with the GRU (the Russian equivalent of the CIA), were:

> *...using human intelligence officers and a variety of technical tools...designated for tampering, altering, or causing a misappropriation of information with the purpose or effect of interfering with the 2016 U.S. election processes.* [4]

As conversation on the internet moved away from the comment sections of message boards to social media platforms like Facebook and Twitter, validation proved even easier to numerically manipulate. With enough troll infrastructure, any opinion had the potential to appear popular and thus, for many readers, legitimate. Since most social networks are programmed by algorithms to automatically promote stories that appear to be popular, the websites ended up becoming complicit in expanding the readership of news stories that would only later be categorized as "fake news." Because of this, Congress would officially reprimand the leading figures of those companies in the years to follow.

While the Russian government's online disinformation campaign may have been the most ambitious, it was not the only one to use internet anonymity to present government views as those of ordinary citizens. In China, city governments began officially hiring online commentators to write supportive posts on web forums, a position that the Chinese Communist Party later officially sanctioned in 2007. Years before Russian trolls began dominating our headlines, the United States Military Central Command began using an "online persona management service" to operate troll accounts issuing pro-American propaganda in Arabic, Farsi, Urdu, and Pashto to purportedly disrupt the online recruitment of suicide bombers in the Middle East. In smaller countries, like Cambodia, political leaders have been accused of purchasing engagement on websites like Facebook in order to evoke the fiction of mass popularity. "Software like this has the potential to destroy the internet as a forum for constructive debate," warned the British activist George Monbiot in 2011.[5]

The internet is ever evolving and will only continue to change with the passage of time. The websites referred to in this volume will give way to new interfaces, populated by dead souls that will, similarly, soon disappear as if they were never there. The conversation will move on in an indeterminate direction, but many of the issues and questions we face today will remain the same. *At Issue: Troll Factories* is a primer that begins in Russia but ends in the United States, covering issues of urgent concern around the world.

Notes

1. "Commissars of the Internet: The FSB at the Computer" by Anna Polyanskaya, Andrei Krivov & Ivan Lomko, *Vestnik Online*, April 30, 2003. Translation: lrtranslations. blogspot.com/2007/02/commissars-of-internet.html

Original article: www.vestnik.com/issues/2003/0430/win/polyanskaya_krivov_lomko.htm

2. The act of writing under a pseudonym of course predates the internet (i.e. the use of a *pen name*), though the internet made it far easier to do, especially on a wider scale.

3. "Effort to Expose Russia's 'Troll Army' Draws Vicious Retaliation," Andrew Higgins, *New York Times*, May 30, 2016.

4. "FACT SHEET: Actions in Response to Russian Malicious Cyber Activity and Harassment" The White House: https://obamawhitehouse.archives.gov/the-press-office/2016/12/29/fact-sheet-actions-response-russian-malicious-cyber-activity-and

5. George Monbiot, "The need to protect the internet from 'astroturfing' grows ever more urgent," *The Guardian*, February 23, 2011.

1

The Establishment of a Troll State

VSquare

VSquare is a journalistic nonprofit and a project of the Reporters' Foundation, a Polish journalistic organization run by Wojciech Cieśla, who writes for Newsweek Polska, *the Polish edition of* Newsweek.

The Russian government's involvement in manipulating online discourse dates to shortly after Putin's election as president, but it has continually changed to accommodate the ever-changing nature of the internet. A money trail is easier to track down. Emails hacked by a Russian branch of Anonymous revealed that, by 2011, the Putin government was spending approximately 290 million RUB ($10 million) per year to influence online discourse in Russia. At first, some of this money went toward paying freelancers to post and promote pro-Putin content on platforms like VKontakte as well as bribing popular bloggers to adopt pro-Putin positions. Later, operations centralized under groups like the Internet Research Agency (IRA), which was ostensibly funded by Yevgeny Prigozhin, a known Putin operative.

Organized groups of pro-Kremlin online commentators have been active for at least 17 years, since the beginning of Vladimir Putin's presidency. In 2003, the name "Kremlin's web brigades" was first used by Russian researchers, Anna Polyanskaya,

"From internet brigades to troll factories," vsquare.org. https://vsquare.org/from-kremlin-web-brigades-to-russian-troll-factories/. Licensed under CC BY 4.0.

Andrey Krivov and Ivan Lomako. Back then, the main purpose of the "brigades" was to praise Vladimir Putin's presidency.

Over the years, "brigades" took upon themselves to do more than just write comments; they started to write blogs with pro-Kremlin propaganda and artificially boost the ratings of pro-Kremlin media materials. That's when they began to operate under Russian special services and political administrators from Kremlin-subordinate Presidential Executive Office.

At the same time, also a new type of companies started to spring up in Russia – partially or wholly dependent on the government, offering services for companies, central and regional institutions, and local governments. Their services consisted of taking care for their clients' positive public image through artificial online activities – often including slandering the clients' competitors and critics.

Despite continuously expanding activities of "Kremlin's web brigades", to this day there is no credible data available on their tasks or numbers during the first decade of existence. It is known that during that time, the brigades were focused on Russian-speaking parts of the internet.

How Much for a Tweet

It was a Russian division of the Anonymous hackers who made it possible to look inside the Kremlin's online propaganda machine for the first time. At the turn of 2011/12, they broke into mailboxes of people connected to the Federal Youth Agency (FYA), including Vasily Yakemenko – the chief of FYA and the first leader of Nashi, a pro-Kremlin youth organization.

The released emails confirm that as early as the beginning of current decade, there was already a powerful army of hired internet users operating in Russia, tasked to increase Vladimir Putin's support ratings. The objective was to carry out discrediting propaganda actions against the opposition and independent media. It was paid for directly by Kremlin from the funds passed on to the Federal Youth Agency, and orchestrated by the chief of FYA

Vasily Yakemenko, under the watchful eye of Vladislav Surkov, Kremlin's propaganda leader.

Thanks to Anonymous hackers, we now know how much money was being allocated towards Internet propaganda: approx. 290 million RUB (10 million USD) per year.

This amount is twelve times higher than publicly known propaganda expenditures of FYA's press office in September 2011. FYA's spendings amounted to 23.6 million RUB (0.8 million USD).

No less than 5.9 million RUB was spent on traditional propaganda: paid articles in printed media (0.38 to 1.2 million RUB per article which equals 13.000 to 40.000 USD) and on most popular websites (12 to 300.000 RUB per article – 400 to 10.000 USD). The rest, ca. 8.61 million RUB (290.000 USD) was spent on more innovative forms of propaganda.

The money has covered such projects as running pro-Putin groups on VKontakte (Russian equivalent of Facebook – at least 2 million RUB = 70.000 USD), pro-Kremlin bloggers (at least 0.7 million RUB – 25.000 USD), Twitter users (at least 0.5 million RUB – 17.000 USD), or active commentators on news websites and social media (at least 1.1 million RUB – 37.000 USD).

Pro-Kremlin bloggers received monthly payments ranging from 4.000 to 30.000 RUB (130-1000 USD), and the more industrious ones would also enjoy free MacBooks an iPads. In order to receive payments and gifts they were required to produce regular reports on their work.

In some exceptional circumstances – whenever it was necessary to bribe a blogger who was popular in independent media or opposition circles – FYA was ready to pay up to 200.000 RUB (7.000 USD) per one pro-Kremlin post. Thanks to government funding, Kremlin managed to take control over content published by hundreds of most popular blogs in whole Russia.

Task-based operation scheme applied to Internet commentators as well. They too had to submit reports on their work to FYA. They were required to comment on articles published on news websites, blogs, and on social media posts, as well as to engage in discussions online. They received daily instructions from their supervisors – on how to praise Putin and slander the opposition.

The norm required to seek reimbursement was 60 comments and 6 discussions a week. Short comments were worth ca. 85 RUB (3 USD), longer comments – 125 RUB (4 USD), and discussions were paid 200 RUB (7 USD) each.

The best players could make as much as 50.000 RUB (1.7000 USD) a month – and an iPad on top of that. However, sometimes FYA would fail to meet its financial obligations, which would lead to conflicts. One of the displeased recruits was a blogger and moderator of a VKontakte group called "I really like Putin". Instead of a bank transfer, he only received a MacBook – so he threatened to curb down pro-Kremlin propaganda.

Emails obtained by Anonymous also reveal the price-list of popular Russian Twitter users.

One tweet cost between 500 and 12000 RUB (12-400 USD).

Eventually, FYA started hiring full-time employees to work as bloggers, commentators, Twitter and Facebook users. They were required to spread information through multiple sources – for example, to run 5 blogs and 5 Twitter and Facebook accounts. According to the revealed emails, most of the employees were young women.

Plans for early 2012 included expanding online propaganda base to 100 full time users, expecting this number to grow even further over time. In order to lower the risk of discovery that all those people are using one computer, all employees were required to use anonymizing proxy servers.

Apart from articles, blogs, posts, tweets and comments, FYA would also finance manipulating of online upvoting by illegal purchases of likes, and fake traffic generators on websites it wanted to promote. This strategy helped to validate their videos on YouTube, pro-Putin blog notes, social media comments, and other propaganda content.

Emails also show strategies in play behind Twitter-bots (they would automatically answer to tweets on certain topics), and bots that would automatically comment on articles posted online. FYA admitted to having control over 20.000 Twitter accounts and another 20.000 blogs it could use for various purposes.

Obtained correspondence proves that FYA employees were convinced that the U.S. and China resort to similar methods in their communication strategies.

In December 2011, mass social protests erupted in Russia in response to rigged parliamentary elections. In the meantime, opposition managed to gain advantage on the Russian-speaking internet. Despite using innovative methods of manipulation and relatively large resources, the Federal Youth Agency's work results were not very impressive.

As consequence of the upheaval, on 27 December 2001 Vladislav Surkov, the man responsible for supervising Russian internet propaganda, was dismissed from his post of government chief-of-staff in the Presidential Executive Office.

Troll Factories Gain Speed

Surkov was replaced by Vyacheslav Volodin. His previous main achievement was the pacification of the largest independent Russian news websites. Volodin didn't forget about Surkov's online projects, but the internet propaganda center was moved from Moscow to the Republic of Adygea (Yablonovsky and Perekatny urban settlements on the suburbs of Krasnodar), Nizhny Novgorod Oblast (a suburban settlement Zelyony Gorod), and St. Petersburg (a suburban settlement Olgino).

The last of three locations has become the most famous Russian "troll factory" in summer 2013. It operates under the name Internet Research Agency (Agentstvo Internet Issledovaniya – AII). Quite soon after it was established, the Agency was hailed the "Ministry of Truth". After just one year AII moved its headquarters to an office building at 55 Savushkina Street, where it remains to this day. We don't know much about two other factories. Neither hackers nor independent journalists have managed to infiltrate their servers so far.

The Internet Research Agency was established and has been funded by Yevgeny Prigozhin, whose career started in catering industry in the 90s. Prigozhin opened an elite restaurant New Island on a riverboat in St. Petersburg, where president Putin celebrated his 50th birthday in 2002. That's when Prigozhin met Putin – it sparked friendship between the two, and helped Prigozhin's career speed up.

Prigozhin became Putin's personal chef and his companies took over catering services in Kremlin; they also started providing food to Russian schools and military bases. The sum of all contracts signed by Prigozhin with the state exceeded 140 billion RUB (ca. 4-5 billion USD).

In late summer 2013 the Internet Research Agency was infiltrated by independent Russian journalists. They were tempted by a job offer looking for "internet operators" responsible for writing comments, social media posts and running blogs for 1200 RUB (30 USD) per day, or 26.000 RUB (650 USD) per month.

In 2014 and 2015 new secrets leaked from the company, released by AII's former employees – some of them had applied for the job in order to discover and publish sensitive information, others were simply unsatisfied with work in AII.

Significant contribution to our knowledge on the mechanisms running Kremlin's propaganda was also made by Russian hackers from Shaltai Boltai group. The hackers stole and published mailboxes of people from AII and connected companies. The main source of information were mailboxes of Olga Dzalba, AII's financial director, and that of Aleman Consulting – a company that analyzed a number of local, national and international media connected to AII. All those projects were financed from the budget of Concord holding company, owned by Yevgeny Prigozhin. Reports from AII activities within respective projects were sent to Vyacheslav Volodin, the new first deputy chief of staff of the Presidential Administration of Russia, responsible for propaganda. This shows that just as Surkov did before him, Volodin had immediate control over the project.

The way AII functioned wasn't much different from the Federal Youth Agency described above. Both entities had the same objective: to manipulate the online image of Russia and the world so the internet users would see them the way Kremlin wanted. AII's budget also covers the cost of cooperation with well-known Russian bloggers and journalists, just like FYA did before. However, they are separated by the scale of their actions. AII's structures are significantly larger and better organized. Apart from Russian speakers, it also employs people specializing in other languages.

According to data available, Yevgeny Prigozhin would spend 40 to 60 million RUB (1 million USD) a month on AII operations. Almost half of this amount was spent on salaries. Initially the company employed 100 people, but each year the numbers grew. In 2014 AII already had 600 employees.

Most of the employees are students, working in 24/7 shifts in specific sections the editorial team was divided into. In order to keep their work secret, employees from respective sections have no contact with each other.

The "Comments" team consists of people whose job is to control ten-odd Facebook, Twitter and VKontakte accounts each, as well as to maintain activity on various forums. They are required to write 100-125 pro-Kremlin comments a day. Profiles vary – they can "belong" to students, blue collar workers or housewives, both from large cities and Russian province.

"Blogger" editorial team is made of people writing at least three blogs each – they are required to reach the daily output of 10-12 posts. The secret "Fake News" editors must rewrite and edit information so it fits pro-Kremlin narrative before it's further spread on AII-controlled websites and social media pages. There is also a "Visual" editorial team that produces propaganda YouTube videos and pro-Kremlin graphics. Over time, the editorial teams expanded and started hiring online employees to carry out similar tasks in English, German, French and Ukrainian. And just like in FYA, the Internet Research Agency employees also have to write detailed reports on their work in order to receive payments.

Released documents include sample reports. One of the writers listed all 182 comments he made on a certain day, split into topics he commented on: opposition, Ministry of Defense, USA, EU, Middle East, Vladimir Putin, Ukraine.

A workday in AII would only begin after employees receive their daily technical tasks. Those tasks are based on articles and news from Russia Today. The tasks refer to events that took place over the past few days or are expected to happen very soon. They usually consist of 3 to 7 topics. In some exceptional cases there could be more (like after the assassination of opposition activist Boris Nemtsov) – during that time, trolls received as much as 26 tasks a day.

The first element of the task is the main idea about the event in question. On 28 February 2015 the idea was: "Nemtsov's assassination was not convenient for Russian authorities, therefore it was an anti-Russian provocation". After that, the thesis was coined: it's possible that Ukrainian politicians were involved in Boris Nemtsov's death. The next step was to include key information in the technical task, meant for AII writers to use in order to make Kremlin's claim more credible. For example: Nemtsov had friends in Ukraine, which is suspicious enough already, and so on.

Other parts of the task are to include links and articles with this information (including foreign materials, if their perspective is in line with Kremlin's propaganda), and keywords that might be used to find the topic on Google or Yandex.

2

Russia's Sense of Self

Stephen Hutchings and Joanna Szostek

Stephen Hutchings is a professor of Russian studies and Director of Research in the School of Arts, Languages and Cultures at the University of Manchester. Joanna Szostek is a postdoctoral fellow at the University College London School of Slavonic and East European Studies.

Russian involvement in Ukraine—which turned into a military invasion in 2014—expanded the Russian government's interest in influencing discourse beyond its own borders. In particular, the Russian Ministry of Foreign Affairs issued a directive targeting its resources toward creating "instruments for influencing how it is perceived in the world." In turn, the Russian government would develop a number of narratives through which its operators would express pro-Putin geopolitical positions. Beyond web brigades, total government control of most media channels permitted these positions to largely go unchallenged inside and outside Russia's borders.

The Russian leadership views mass communication as a crucial arena of global politics, in which rival powers work to undermine each other and further their own interests at others' expense. The ability to project narratives to foreign audiences is

"Dominant Narratives in Russian Political and Media Discourse during the Ukraine Crisis" by Stephen Hutchings and Joanna Szostek, April 28,2015. Reprinted by permission.

therefore considered a matter of national security, as is the ability to control the circulation of narratives at home. In its Foreign Policy Concept of 2013, Russia declared that it must 'create instruments for influencing how it is perceived in the world', 'develop its own effective means of information influence on public opinion abroad', and 'counteract information threats to its sovereignty and security' (Russian Foreign Ministry, 2013). In line with these goals, the Russian government has invested heavily in media resources that can convey its point of view to other countries, such as the TV news channel RT.

Meanwhile, independent and critical voices have been increasingly stifled within Russia's domestic media environment. State control over news on the main television channels (Pervyy Kanal, Rossiya 1, NTV) has been tight for years – all of them reflect and support the government's stance. There is still pluralism in the press, on the radio, and on the Internet. However, the Ukraine crisis has coincided with a clampdown even in these 'freer' parts of Russia's media landscape: the popular news website lenta.ru has had its editorial team replaced and the Internet and satellite channel Dozhd has been evicted from its premises.

The narratives described in this chapter can be observed throughout the Russian media which are aligned with the state – from state-owned federal channels to commercial tabloids like *Komsomolskaya Pravda* and the widely-used state news agency/website RIA Novosti. Some of the narratives have caused considerable consternation in Kiev. The post-Yanukovych Ukrainian government quickly banned Russian channels from Ukrainian cable networks, fearing that tendentious Russian reporting was stoking unrest in the eastern regions. It has certainly caused widespread offence in other parts of the country. Ukraine has set up a Ministry of Information in an attempt to 'repel Russia's media attacks' (Interfax-Ukraine, 2014). The conflict in Ukraine has thus become an 'information war' as much as a conventional one.

Narratives of 'the West', the USA and the EU

Anti-western narratives […]attribute various negative characteristics to the USA and EU states via an interrelated set of plotlines that explain current developments with reference to 'historical' patterns. Negative narratives about the West serve the goals of the Russian leadership in a number of ways: they diminish the credibility of western criticism of Russia, they legitimise Russian behaviour in the eyes of the public, and they defend Russia's self-identity as a European great power. At the same time, the narratives frame how Russians at all levels of society, including the elite, interpret world politics. Therefore, the fact that they are used instrumentally to bolster support for the Russian authorities should not obscure the fact that the narratives have also been internalised among those in authority and thus influence the direction of policy.

Characteristics attributed to western governments by the Russian media include hypocrisy, risibility, arrogant foolishness, and a lack of moral integrity to the point of criminality. Russian television finds evidence of these characteristics in events both past and present. At one point in summer 2014, for example, it referred back to US President Woodrow Wilson promoting democracy and self-determination 'just for export' while denying rights to African and Native Americans. The presenter claimed that the USA had demanded 'the right to judge everyone by its own very flexible standards for a hundred years' (Rossiya 1, 2014). Such claims undermine the validity of international condemnations of Russian actions in Ukraine by conveying that those doing the condemning have only their own selfish interests at heart – not any real moral values.

'Double standards' (*dvoynyye standarty*) is a charge that is levelled against the West time and time again by the Russian state media as they report and echo the words of the Russian president, foreign minister, and other officials. President Vladimir Putin, for instance, pointed out that American troops and military bases were all over the world, 'settling the fates of other nations while thousands of kilometres from their own borders'. This makes it 'very strange', he argued, that the Americans should denounce Russian foreign troop deployments so much smaller than their own (Putin, 2014). Not only does such a line of argument again attack the moral standing of Russia's critics, it also implies, through a comparison of Russian actions with 'similar' American actions, that Russia is just behaving as great powers do – for few doubt the USA's great power status.

The Russian media frequently mocks western leaders and officials for their lack of understanding and for making foolish errors. When Putin gave an interview to French journalists, a Russian presenter said the president had 'patiently and politely engaged in tackling illiteracy, as if warming up ahead of meetings with colleagues from America and Europe' (Rossiya 1, 2014a). Sometimes the mockery is personal. US State Department spokeswoman Jen Psaki became a target, with Russian television alleging that internet users had adopted the word 'psaking' to mean issuing categorical statements without first checking their accuracy (Rossiya 1, 2014b). The implication is clearly that condemnation of Russia originating from such sources should not be taken seriously.

The Russian media do differentiate, however, between the USA and Europe. The USA is more often accused of outright criminality. Over summer 2014, US 'war crimes' in Ukraine were highlighted regularly and the charges reinforced through parallels with history. In June, for instance, a Russian presenter claimed:

> *Ten years ago the Americans used white phosphorous against people in the Iraqi town of Fallujah. Afterwards the White House lied that it hadn't done so... Now the USA is covering up its accomplices in the criminal deployment of incendiary ammunition in Ukraine. (Rossiya 1, 2014c)*

A report about the tragic crash of flight MH17 similarly observed that there had been only a few cases of the military shooting down civilian aircraft, but the most serious had been

Iranian Air flight 655, downed by the US Air Force in 1988, for which 'America didn't even apologise' (Rossiya 1, 2014d).

European states, on the other hand, were generally portrayed as being led astray against their own best interests by malign American influence. Russian Foreign Minister Sergey Lavrov claimed that international attempts to 'restrict Russia's possibilities' were led primarily by the USA, not the European powers; he argued that the Americans were 'trying to prevent Russia and the EU from uniting their potentials' due to their goal of 'retaining global leadership' (Lavrov, 2014). According to Russian television, the sanctions imposed on Moscow were forced through by the USA 'to weaken the Europeans along with the Russians and get them hooked on [American] shale gas' (Rossiya 1, 2014e). Germany and France are the countries which – in the Russian narrative – the USA is particularly desperate to prevent drawing closer to Russia. Around the anniversary of the outbreak of World War I, Russian television again drew on history to make its point, reporting:

> *Then, as now, Germany and Russia were acquiring strength. With their peaceful cooperation, the old world had every chance for prosperity and influence. Then, as now, the English and Americans had a common goal – to sow discord between Russia and Germany and in doing so, exhaust them. Then, as now, willingness to destroy part of the Orthodox world was used to bring Russia into a big war. Then, it was Serbia, now it is eastern Ukraine. (Rossiya 1, 2014f)*

This plotline is used to suggest that Russia and Europe would enjoy a close and untroubled relationship were it not for American interference. Tensions with the EU can thus be accounted for without having to acknowledge any fundamental differences that might threaten Russia's European sense of self.

When used strategically in an international context, narratives 'integrate interests and goals – they articulate end states and suggest how to get there' (Miskimmon, O'Loughlin, and Roselle, 2013, p. 5). Three dominant plotlines point particularly to the Russian leadership's goals vis-à-vis western countries. The first relates to western 'interference' causing instability around the world. This plotline situates unrest and violence in Iraq, Syria, Libya, Afghanistan, Georgia, Ukraine, and elsewhere all within the same explanatory paradigm: the West (led by the USA) gets involved, then countries fall apart. The resolution proposed – either implicitly or explicitly – is for the West (above all the USA) to adopt a less interventionist foreign policy. Russia's desire to see the USA less involved in the domestic affairs of other states relates particularly to Ukraine and the post-Soviet region, but extends similarly to parts of the world where Russia's comfortable and profitable dealings with entrenched autocratic leaders (Saddam Hussein, Muammar Gaddafi, Bashar al-Assad) have been disrupted by American support for such leaders' removal.

A second goal-oriented plotline relates to the West (above all the USA) seeking global dominance and acting without due consultation with others. The logical resolution to this plotline favoured by the Russian leadership is to grant non-western countries such as Russia (or perhaps, more accurately, Russia and those who agree with Russia) a greater say in international decision-making. This goal is expressed in Russian calls for 'multipolarity' and endorsement of formats such as BRICS and the G20.

A third major goal-oriented plotline relates to the 'inevitable' continuation of Russia's cooperation with Europe. The narrative projected by Russian leaders and state media insists that commercial and business ties between Russia and the EU are continuing to develop, despite political tensions, because both sides have so much to gain from 'pragmatic cooperation'. The end state which Russia's leaders envisage to resolve security problems in Europe is a 'single economic and humanitarian space from Lisbon to Vladivostok' (a space which obviously attaches Europe to Russia while detaching it from the USA) (Putin, 2014a).

All these Russian goals are associated with the Russian state's preferred identity as a European great power. By opposing western 'interference' abroad, the Russian leadership hopes to block political changes – particularly in the post-Soviet region – which might diminish the international influence which it 'must', as a great power, exert. By rejecting international formats in which Russia's preferences are overridden in favour of formats where Russia's voice is louder (e.g. BRICS), the Russian leadership is claiming the right to be heeded, which great powers 'must' enjoy. By pushing for greater economic cooperation with the EU and promoting the idea of a common space from Lisbon to Vladivostok, Russia is asserting its membership of Europe, while striving to minimise Europe's 'western-ness' – the aspect of Europe's identity that connects with the USA and excludes Russia.

Narratives of Russian Nationhood

The narratives by which Russia projects its position on Ukraine in the international arena are inextricably linked to the grand nation-building mission that has been underway on the domestic stage since the tail end of the El'tsyn era, and which has intensified significantly under Putin. It must be remembered that, unlike other post-Soviet nations (including Ukraine), when communism fell in 1991, Russia's centuries-long history as the core of a larger, imperial entity ended abruptly, and it was left with no clear sense of what it was, of its 'natural' boundaries and basis for 'belonging', or of its key national myths. The fact that remnants of its former imperial conquests (including the Muslim regions of the North Caucasus) remained within its borders, and that Russia is still a vast, multi-ethnic, multi-lingual country, have not made the task of answering those questions any easier.

It is unsurprising, therefore, that the anti-westernism that has recently defined Russia's post-Ukraine international stance, and that has recurred periodically throughout Russia's history, has also dominated its domestic nation-building programme. Crucially, it has been at the heart of efforts to establish the basis for national belonging. This was crystallised in the extensively reported address that Putin gave to the two houses of the Russian Duma following the annexation of Crimea. One of the most striking lines of the speech made reference to 'a fifth column… a disparate bunch of "national traitors" with which the West now appears to be threatening Russia' (Putin, 2014b). The reference to 'national traitors', a term associated with the Stalin-era repressions, had a chilling effect on Russia's now beleaguered opposition movement, but it was in keeping with the scapegoating of west-leaning liberals and other marginal groups that had been growing over the past two years. The label soon gained currency among prominent pro-Kremlin television commentators. During a special edition of the *Voskresnyi vecher* programme broadcast on the Rossiya channel on 21 March 2014, and in response to a question from the host, Vladimir Solovev, Dmitrii Kiselev attributed his inclusion in the list of individuals named in western sanctions against Russia to the actions of such national traitors (Kiselev, 2014).

It is commonly assumed that the anti-US and anti-European hysteria which gripped the Russian public sphere in 2014 is attributable solely to a Kremlin strategy implemented with an iron hand and from the top down. However, this is not entirely the case. First, Russia is not the Soviet Union, and certain prominent media figures linked to (but not necessarily coincident with) the Kremlin line are given the freedom to develop Kremlin thinking to extremes well beyond what might be permissible in official circles. When punitive sanctions were imposed on Russia, Kiselev was at the centre of a frenzy of cold-war rhetoric, using the platform of his *Vesti nedeli* programme to point out that Russia alone among nations has the capacity to turn the USA into 'radioactive dust' (Rossiya 1, 2014h). He was echoed by extreme right-wing writer Aleksandr Prokhanov, like Kiselev a frequent presence on Russian television, who announced that his 15-year-long dream of a return to the Cold War had been fulfilled (Barry, 2014). The two commentators, both close to Putin's inner circle, offer a sobering demonstration of the dependency of Russian national pride in its distortive, Putinesque manifestation on the 'treacherous, conspiratorial West' that in the aftermath of the Ukraine crisis is Russia's constant nemesis.

Secondly, Kremlin thinking itself is developed in part in response to, and under the influence of, ideological currents circulating at a level below that of official discourse, which employs the state-aligned media to 'mainstream' those currents and thus legitimate the accommodations it makes with them. In the months following the annexation of Crimea and the peak of hostilities in Eastern Ukraine, for example, the Eurasianist and extreme nationalist Aleksandr Dugin, who has been influential in shaping official discourse, once again stalked Russian talk shows. He had been somewhat sidelined prior to this and his re-emergence was an indicator of the new pathway the Russian political elite had now embarked upon. In an interview with the well-known presenter Vladimir Pozner, Dugin advocated the outright invasion of Ukraine by Russia (Dugin, 2014).

Dugin's account of Russia as the leader of a powerful union of Slavic and Central Asian states capable of reconciling Islam and Christianity is only one of a set of core ideological narratives with which news and current affairs programmes are framed. In addition, there is the isolationist Russian nationalism[1] which rails against migration, privileging the status of ethnic Russians and showing little interest in engagement beyond Russia's borders. This competes with an imperialist variant that is nostalgic for the Soviet Union and keen to preserve the Russian Federation as a multicultural state. Finally, a narrative[2] has emerged positing Russia as a global standard bearer for 'traditional values', with either an Orthodox Christian, or a dual Orthodox and Muslim, inflexion. Each carries its own brand of anti-western sentiment and each has its champions on Russian state-aligned television. The Kremlin has sometimes struggled to navigate these narratives, but in justifying Russia's actions in Crimea and Eastern Ukraine, Putin succeeded in blending several of them, bringing one or more of them to the fore for particular purposes.

The pretext for Russia's actions in Crimea, and later for both its tacit and its explicit support for the separatist rebels in Eastern Ukraine, focused on the protection of its 'compatriots' (*sootechestvenniki*). The conflation of this term with 'ethnic Russians' (*etnicheskie russkie*) and 'Russian speakers' (*russkoiazychnye*) reflects the ethnicisation of national identity characteristic of isolationists such as Arkadii Mamontov, host of *Rossiia's Spetsialnyi* correspondent show. But the 'compatriots' theme also had resonance for pseudo-imperialists like Prokhanov and the Eurasianist Dugin. News broadcasts, including Channel 1's *Novosti*, gave sympathetic treatment to demonstrations throughout Russia and called to endorse the resistance of Russian speakers in Crimea and the Donetsk and Luhansk regions of Ukraine to the new Kiev authorities. The demonstrators' slogans and demands were quoted at length:

> *Russia doesn't abandon its own'; 'Sevastopol – we are with you'...*
> *with slogans like this the inhabitants of Petropavlovsk came to a*
> *meeting in support of their compatriots. They spoke both Russian*
> *and Ukrainian... 'We Ukrainians are with the Russians; we are*
> *one country, one nation; we have both Ukrainian and Russian*
> *blood in us; there is no separate Ukraine and no separate Russia'...*
> *'The fraternal people of Ukraine are connected to us historically,*
> *culturally and by their spiritual values. Our grandfathers and*
> *great grandfathers fought together on the front and liberated our*
> *great Soviet Union. (Channel 1, 2014)*

The different forms of nationalism did not always work in harmony, however, as illustrated by shifts and contradictions in coverage of the resistance of the Muslim Tatar popular to the annexation of Crimea. Some pre-annexation news broadcasts acknowledged the Tatar community's unease about the possibility of a Russian takeover, even including open admissions that many Crimean Tatars were not pro-Russian. Later broadcasts echoed Putin's triumphal annexation speech which insisted (against all the evidence) that most Crimean Tatars supported reunification with Russia. In this representation, the Crimean Tatars were used as a symbol of Crimea's and Russia's unity in diversity. This ambivalent recognition and simultaneous denial of the 'Crimean Tatar problem' exposed the tension between Putin's neo-imperialist/Eurasianist variant on Russian patriotism (one which, like its nineteenth and twentieth century predecessors, aspires to square the need for inclusivity and inter-ethnic harmony with the imperative to maintain the dominant ethnic group's power), and the isolationist nationalists, for whom 'Muslim minorities' constitute a problem.

The slogans quoted above were indicative of a further powerful narrative of nationhood driving Russian media responses to the consequences of regime change in Ukraine: the myth of the Great Patriotic War and the shared struggle of the Russian and Ukrainian peoples against fascism. This in turn was linked to the purported role of Nazi extremists in the Euromaidan movement and the new Ukrainian regime. Accusations that the new Kiev regime is packed with, tolerant of, or manipulated by Nazi extremists have continued to remain at the centre of Russian media accounts of the Euromaidan uprising and their efforts to discredit and de-legitimise the post-Yanukovich government and its actions. Emotive references to *Banderovtsy* (followers of the Ukrainian war-time Nazi collaborator Stepan Bandera) abounded in the discourse not only of media commentators, but Russian political leaders including Putin himself. Pro-Kremlin outlets have consistently emphasised the role of volunteer soldiers from the right-wing *Pravy sektor* in prosecuting Kiev's 'punitive operation' in Eastern Ukraine.

As recently as November 2014, the Rossiia television channel was reporting on meetings at which all elements of the Russian political mainstream recalled the shared memories of the victory against Hitler and united against the threat of Ukrainian Nazism. On 4 November, it broadcast a story about a political rally organised to coincide with Russia's 'Day of National Unity' and attended by the Communist Party, the Kremlin-aligned United Russia Party, Zhirinovskii's Liberal Democratic Party, and the social democratic Just Russia Party. All four leaders were reported to have condemned fascist extremism at the heart of the new Ukraine (Zhirinovsky, Ziuganov, and Mironov, 2014).

Finally, however, the anti-fascist agenda coexists in an uneasy relationship with the links that the Kremlin has been forging with far-right forces throughout Europe (and indeed the USA) as part of its efforts to promote Russia as the world leader of 'traditional, conservative values'. Russia's endorsement of the nuclear family and the Orthodox Church, its antagonism to non-standard sexualities, and its scorn for 'politically correct', liberal tolerance of difference have resonated with the likes of Marine Le Pen in France, Tea Party supporter Pat Buchanan in the US, and Nigel Farage's UKIP in Britain. The visceral opposition of many of these groups to the EU, and to the entire 'European project', helps explain the support they have expressed for the Russian position on Ukraine and official Russian media outlets have not been slow to capitalise on this. Nigel Farage has appeared 17 times on Russia's international television channel, RT (Russia Today), since December 2010, and his relationship with it has come under scrutiny in the UK press. But as *The Guardian* points out, sympathy for Russia is not limited to the margins of British politics:

> *Farage's views on the EU's role in the Ukraine are shared by some Tory Eurosceptic MPs. In a Bruges Group film on how the EU has blundered in the Ukraine, John Redwood says: "The EU seems to be flexing its words in a way that Russia finds worrying and provokes Russia into flexing its military muscles". (Wintour and Mason, 2014)*

What might seem the most paradoxical and counter-intuitive of allegiances is, in fact, just one illustration of the multiple ideological reversals and realignments that are the continuing aftermath of the collapse of communism and the ending of the Cold War.

Conclusions

One conclusion we might draw from our survey of the Russian media response to the Ukraine crisis is that Russian tactics in what some have called the 'New Cold War' should not be attributed to a purely cynical eclecticism (exploiting whichever political and ideological currents and trends that serve current needs, no matter what their provenance). Although such eclecticism is apparent, we should not ignore the (so far unsuccessful) efforts to knit the dominant narratives, despite all their many contradictions, into an ideological fabric capable of providing the basis for a coherent worldview and a stable sense of national identity. Nor should the notion of an all-out 'information war' between Russia and the West, and the way it is used to justify any manner of distortion by omission, exaggeration, or sometimes downright untruth, be seen outside the context of the residual influence of the Leninist approach to media objectivity as a 'bourgeois construct', or of a reaction against established values of impartiality and objectivity that extends well beyond Russia (Wintour and Mason, 2014).

However, and in a further challenge to received wisdom on Russian media coverage of Ukraine, the development of the post-Ukraine Russian world view is not an entirely top-down process and betrays the influence of powerful sub-official and popular discourses, which must be alternatively appropriated, moderated, and reconciled with one another, and with the official line. Rather than a passive tool in the Kremlin's hands, the state-aligned media are at times serving as an active agent in managing this process.

It would be wrong, too, to explain Russia's actions and their mediation by pro-Kremlin press and broadcasting outlets as those of an aggressive, expansionist nation determined to extend its sphere of influence into new areas. Rather, they reflect the perception of a threat to what Russia sees as its rightful status as a great power, and to its current regional interests (however distorted and misplaced we may believe those interests to be). Finally, the visceral anti-western rhetoric that dominates Russia's public sphere to its inevitable detriment is not as undifferentiated as is often suggested; ultimately, Russia continues to harbour the desire to be seen as a European nation and as part of a continental bulwark against untrammelled American hegemony.

The correctives we propose to more reductive accounts of Russian media coverage of Ukraine do not diminish the reprehensibility of Russia's apparent willingness to flout both international law and basic standards of objectivity in news reporting. Nonetheless, the roots of the current crisis over Ukraine cannot be fully understood without appreciating the nuances, origins, and complexities of the media narratives by which Russia attempts to legitimate its behaviour.

Notes

[1] http://www.thenation.com/article/176956/how-russian-nationalism-fuels-race-riots

[2] http://www.thedailybeast.com/articles/2014/06/29/iraq-s-christians-see-putin-as-savior.html

3

Information as a Weapon

Chris Collison

Chris Collison is pursuing a master's degree in international studies at the Ellison Center for Russian, East European, and Central Asian Studies at the Henry M. Jackson School of International Studies.

In 2016, Putin accused the United States of undermining regional stability in Eastern Europe, putting into legal language his longstanding campaign to "strengthen the position of the Russian Federation's means of mass information and mass communication" in retaliation. The approach that Russia's web brigades would ultimately take can be traced to the work of an influential Kremlin-affiliated political figure named Aleksandr Dugin, who has often likened himself to American alt-right blogger and former Trump advisor Steve Bannon. Dugin is credited in this viewpoint for developing the concept of using the internet to mobilize information as a weapon. This is the fundamental logic of the web brigade: sowing confusion in the mist of political tumult.

The extent of Russian meddling in American politics in 2016 shocked political commentators and journalists and has raised fears of a new kind of information war, but to those who have observed prior Russian behavior, these hacks and media smears appear to be part of a broader information strategy that Russia has been executing against Ukraine, the European Union, NATO, and

"Russia's Information War: Old Strategies, New Tools," by Chris Collison. Reprinted by permission.

the United States since the outbreak of the Euromaidan protest movement in 2013. That strategy has its roots in information warfare techniques developed in Soviet times and then adapted for contemporary domestic and international purposes following the election of Vladimir Putin in 2000. Building on Soviet deception strategy, Russia uses a network of freelance cyber warriors and homegrown ideologues to distance itself from actions against Western and Ukrainian interests.

[...]

Sources of Russia's Information Policy

The origins of Russia's current information warfare strategy can be traced at least as far back as the 1990s, when the Russian National Security Council identified the growing need to address information as a commodity in the digital age. But perhaps the most revealing move was the state's adoption of the Doctrine of Information Security in 2000. This wide-ranging document lays out in no uncertain terms the Russian government's goal of securing what it calls the growing "information sphere," a catch-all term that includes essentially every aspect of communications and means of communications, including information infrastructure, entities engaged in the collection and dissemination of information, and systems governing public relations (Government of Russia 2000). The document articulates the need to promote a positive image of Russia abroad as a key component of foreign policy. It also explains that information security is a high priority for protecting Russian national interests and the interests of Russian society.

The hierarchical and secretive nature of Russian decision-making means it is extremely difficult to determine exactly what considerations go into information warfare policy when put into practice, but Russian military and security documents give some clues as to how media policy and technology is viewed from a military perspective. These documents, which have been revised several times since Putin assumed the presidency in 1999, offers insight into what strategies are prioritized and how the restructuring of the military and the development of new tools has influenced information warfare policy over time.

The origins of Russia's current information warfare strategy can be traced at least as far back as the 1990s, when the Russian National Security Council identified the growing need to address information as a commodity in the digital age. But perhaps the most revealing move was the state's adoption of the Doctrine of Information Security in 2000. This wide-ranging document lays out in no uncertain terms the Russian government's goal of securing what it calls the growing "information sphere," a catch-all term that includes essentially every aspect of communications and means of communications, including information infrastructure, entities engaged in the collection and dissemination of information, and systems governing public relations (Government of Russia 2000). The document articulates the need to promote a positive image of Russia abroad as a key component of foreign policy. It also explains that information security is a high priority for protecting Russian national interests and the interests of Russian society.

Although it declares Russia's intent to protect freedom of speech and other constitutional rights in several short passages, the document identifies a long list of potential threats to information security and to Russian society more broadly. From this document, it is clear that the Russian government in 2000 saw itself in a vulnerable position globally and internally in terms of both its conventional military capabilities and in the growing digital information sphere. The document emphasizes threats to what the state saw as Russian spirituality. For example: "threats to... Russia's spiritual revival; depreciation of spiritual values, the propaganda of specimens of mass culture based on the cult of violence or on spiritual and moral values contrary to the values adopted in Russian society." (Government of Russia 2000). Even before Vladimir Putin's consolidation of power in the coming years, his early government made protecting Russia's "spiritual" culture—a key component of Russia's new nationalism—a priority for information security.

The doctrine also identifies what it terms the vulnerability of Russian citizens in the information sphere, claiming that civil society and the legal system in Russia are weak and that citizens are threatened by "information manipulation" meant to "evoke a negative reaction among people, which in a number of cases leads to a destabilization of the social and political situation in society."[1] It defines information manipulation as disinformation, information concealment, and distortion. It also warns of the influence of foreign media and media owned by foreign companies and identifies the need to address the "uncontrolled expansion of the foreign media sector in the national information space." So while the document declares Russia's intention to protect free speech, it also suggests that the lawlessness of information space is having a negative effect on stability and that the state has a responsibility to respond to this threat, foreshadowing repressive measures against domestic mass media that would follow in the coming years.

The threats to Russian society identified in the document are understood to be both internal and external. Coming on the heels of the Second Chechen War and the ensuing insurgency, the document specifically deems it necessary to "not allow for propaganda or campaigning that serves to foment social, racial, national or religious hatred and strife" and the "possible disturbance of social stability...as a result of activities by religious associations preaching religious fundamentalism as well as by totalitarian religious sects." It then moves to external threats, which it identifies chiefly as attempts by "a number of countries toward dominance and the infringement of Russia's interests in the world information space and to oust it from external and domestic markets."

These are reiterated in subsequent policy documents, including the Russian Military Doctrine of 2010. Adopted a decade after the Doctrine on Information Security, the Russian military doctrine identifies a number of "instruments" for protecting Russia's national interests, including information (Government of Russia 2010). Like the 2000 document, it identifies both external and internal dangers but this time specifically names NATO and "the desire...to move the military infrastructure of NATO member countries closer to the borders of the Russian Federation, including expanding the bloc" and "attempts to destabilize the situation in individual states and regions and to undermine strategic stability." This is worth noting because it is strikingly similar to the type of language used by both Russian officials and Russian media in describing Ukraine's 2013-2014 revolution and in the Kremlin's justification for its invasion and 6 annexation of Crimea in March 2014.

"Concepts of Foreign Policy of the Russian Federation," a Ministry of Foreign Affairs policy doctrine signed by President Putin on November 30, 2016, explicitly singles out the United States and its allies for trying to "contain Russia by using political economic, information, and other influences to undermine regional and global stability." It again calls for Russia to "strengthen the position of the Russian Federation's means of mass information and mass communication in the global information space and its means of communicating to the international community Russian perspectives on international processes." (Government of Russia (b) 2016). Curiously, both the Information Security Doctrine of 2000 and the 2010 Military Doctrine define information operations as something to be conducted during peacetime and as a prelude to war, rather than just a component of war itself (Heickero 2010). The view of information operations as a peacetime operation and the desire to communicate Russian perspectives on international processes are implemented as policy through Russia's various state-controlled media platforms such as RT and Sputnik, which the Kremlin has tried to position as big players in the conversation over international events.

Finally, in December 2016 Putin signed the latest Doctrine of Information Security of Russia. The document builds on previous military and information security doctrines, this time asserting the need to balance Russians' need for free information and the needs of national information security—further emphasizing the state's policy of putting security ahead of civil liberties. The document also claims that Russian media is "subject to blatant discrimination abroad" and again emphasizes the need to portray a positive image of Russia internationally (Government of Russia 2016). While US media in 2016 focused primarily on cyber operations prior to Trump's election, Russian policy documents make it clear that such operations are understood to be only one piece of information warfare. The obsession with the "information sphere," the influence of foreign news media, and means to promote a positive image abroad show that the Kremlin prioritizes a multi-faceted strategy that emphasizes information as a way to promote political goals.

Clues from Domestic Practice: New Nationalism

Russia's domestic media began to tilt toward conservatives during the early- to mid- 2000s. Charles Clover describes how Putin's embrace of "information technology" helped rally support for the Putin regime and aided in developing a new nationalism in the country as it emerged from the chaos of the 1990s. According to Clover, the Kremlin was both responding to popular will by constantly monitoring public opinion, which was becoming more nationalist as standards of living rose, and insulating the Kremlin from the public by slowly subduing news media and opposition political parties. Through this activity, social conservatives and nationalist were empowered and became more visible as Putin consolidated power.

Citing conversations with Aleksandr Dugin, a flamboyant political theorist sometimes described as a neo-fascist, Clover describes how Putin aide Vladislav Surkov helped develop a system that simulated pluralism in Russia during the 2000s through the use of shrewd media manipulation and by running "invented" political parties and youth organization. The system amounted to a "postmodernistic pseudo-democracy." He brought together a team of "private political consultants, pollsters, provocateurs, and pocket politicians" to run a made-for-TV political circus that kept Putin's ratings high.[2] Surkov, who spent time working in the advertising industry, helped develop the Russian media landscape as it is now, using what Clover calls "clever puns and inherently contradictory Orwellian wordplays—such as 'sovereign democracy,' illiberal capitalism' and 'managed nationalism.'" Dugin claims Surkov helped him develop his nationalist political party, Rodina, but made sure to never allow it to grow too large or influential. Surkov, it is worth noting, is believed to be a key architect of the Kremlin's strategy to destabilize Eastern Ukraine and set up the so-called Luhansk and Donetsk People's Republics in 2014.[3] Documents leaked in October 2016 by Ukrainian hackers further implicate Surkov in stage-managing the events in the Donbas.[4]

Aleksandr Dugin is among the most prolific and visible political theorists in modern-day Russia, known especially for his book, *The Fourth Political Theory*. In that book, he rejects what he defines as the first three political theories: Liberal democracy (Atlanticism), Marxism-Leninism, and fascism. According to Dugin, the world has entered a phase of "postmodernity" and Russia and the components of its former empire should adopt a "fourth political theory" as an alternative to the three that characterized the 20th century. To Dugin, Western culture is a "local and contemporary phenomenon" and each civilization should build their societies on their particular "internal values." In this, he asks Russia to embrace a unique "Neo-Eurasian" identity and history. While he is unable to describe exactly what a fourth political theory would entail for his country, it is clearly a rejection of globalism, which he sees as imperialism by the West against the traditional values and interests of Russia and "Eurasia."

It is unclear exactly how influential Dugin's ideas are among Russian policymakers and the Russian public, but his positions tend to be largely compatible with those practiced by the Putin regime, and he has a large following online. Earlier, he was recruited by Gleb Pavlovsky for a role on the First National television channel and he has written editorials in major Russian newspapers.[5] Jolanta Darczewska describes Dugin and his network of online contacts and web projects as groups of "spiritual colonies" that bring together like-minded university students and sympathizers abroad. He describes Dugin's network as one of a number of "swarms" that is able to mobilize and promote the Kremlin's talking points.[6] This phenomenon mirrors Russia's cyber strategy, which uses freelancers and outsourced botnets that are not employed directly by the Kremlin for trolling and hacking.[7]

Just days before the vote on Crimean annexation in March 2014, Dugin published an article on his Eurasian Youth Union website entitled, "The Rules of Polemics with the Internal Enemy: A Few Rules of Polemics in New Russia [Novorossiya] (After Crimea)." In the article he writes, "We oppose the US, NATO, and liberalism." He then calls for a "system of synonyms to be used in polemics" to fight "THOSE WHO ARE NOT US." He also calls for new online tactics to be implemented, including "patriotic trolling software, demotivators, memes, and viral videos."[8] Remarkably, his article calls for the very information warfare tactics the Kremlin would use that spring during the outbreak of war in eastern Ukraine and during the US Presidential election two years later.

[…]

By allowing a network of nationalist groups to grow and flourish, the Putin regime is able to distance itself from their activities, maintaining its policy of plausible deniability and obscuring the state's role in mobilization and propaganda efforts.

Disinformation and Weaponized Information: Old Strategy, New Tools

News media have largely settled on the term "hybrid warfare" to describe the Kremlin's strategy against Ukraine over the past three years—first to describe its deployment of unmarked troops, its use of covert operations, and the persistent and disciplined denials of Russian military presence in Ukraine, and then later to describe any act of aggression, including cyber attacks and "weaponized" information, a term used by Peter Pomerantsev and Michael Weiss in late 2014 (Pomerantsev and Weiss 2014). "Hybrid warfare" became a catch-all for Russia's aggression against Ukraine, with one Washington Post article citing Army Gen. Martin E. Dempsey, the chairman of the Joint Chiefs of Staff, warning of future "hybrid conflicts" (Gibbons-Neff 2015). But non-conventional warfare is nothing new, and neither is the idea of "hybrid warfare." As British security expert Keir Giles points out, what we understand today as hybrid war has been used throughout history, especially during various Soviet military campaigns in countries such as Afghanistan, Spain, Egypt, Vietnam, and Korea. He writes that "the blurring of boundaries between peace and war is by now also no novelty" (Giles 2016).

A key component of the news media's definition of hybrid warfare is "weaponized information" or "weaponized media." But information warfare is also not a new concept, and Russia has a long history of waging war by non-military means, especially through the use of deception and false information. While false and misleading reports from Russian media and government officials confused and distracted the Western press during the early stages of the Russia-Ukraine conflict, a look at Soviet policy can shed light on contemporary information warfare techniques. In many ways, the information war Russia has waged against Ukraine and the West is an old strategy adapted for contemporary technology.

The Kremlin has long sought information dominance inside and beyond its borders using a variety of tools that were adapted for the times. Some of these strategies were employed even during the early days of the Soviet Union. Vladimir Lenin spoke of the power of propaganda and agitation in his revolutionary writings, including in *What is to be Done?* (Lenin 1961). Lenin's texts would be studied and poured over by Soviet citizens for more than 70 years, and his strategies adapted, expanded, and perverted to fit the needs of the state and its foreign and domestic intelligence branches. From the Russian Civil War to the Cold War, acts of political deception were key components of communist foreign policy. Chief among the tools developed by the Kremlin was *disinformation*, a word that has entered the international lexicon but is not always well understood in the West. Disinformation is not the same as *misinformation*, or false information that is deliberately intended to deceive, which is sometimes given as the direct translation of the Russian word *dezinfomatsiya* (дезинформация). Disinformation is a deliberate deception technique meant to achieve a political goal (OED Online 2016, Bittman 1985).

[…]

Mass Disinformation: The Rise of RT

While disinformation is not a new strategy, the post-communist period offers numerous avenues for its spread that weren't available during the Cold War. The dominant means of spreading information abroad during the Soviet era was through print and broadcast media, which were expensive and ineffective at achieving mass penetration in foreign media markets. State-run radio stations such as Voice of Moscow and Radio Comintern as well as publications such as the *Morning Star* newspaper never posed serious competition to the diverse and competitive press in the US and Europe. But cable television and the internet have helped to democratize information and have made it cost effective to achieve a great deal of exposure in ways that weren't possible before the collapse of communism.

[…]

RT's willingness to host political figures who would have otherwise had trouble finding air time on major US networks helped it build an audience with the politically marginalized on both the right and the left. Ron Paul, a libertarian who rose to prominence online during the 2008 presidential election, was a frequent guest, as was WikiLeaks founder Julian Assange, who even hosted his own show in 2012 (Stanley 2012). Jared Taylor, a white nationalist who has been identified as a voice of the so-called "alt-right," was also a frequent guest on RT, where he could be found complaining about being marginalized in the mainstream news media, criticizing affirmative action, and warning of growing racism toward white Americans.[9]

[…]

Competing Narratives, but Reaching the Same Conclusion

[…]

So-called "alternative" media proved willing to repeat Kremlin talking points, cherrypicking the aspects of these two competing narratives that best fit their ideological leanings. That the Russian narrative was inherently contradictory when taken as a whole (a globalist liberal effort to support fascist nationalists) didn't seem to matter, as alternative media outlets were willing to run with the parts of the story that advanced their particular ideological goals. Writers from left-wing publications such as Alternet were even featured in more reputable liberal outlets such as Salon, which published an article accusing US Senator John McCain and the State Department of backing neo-Nazis in Ukraine during the Euromaidan revolution (Blumenthal 2014). Left-leaning blogs such as Truthdig also ran with the narrative that the uprising in Ukraine was a far-right conspiracy supported by the west, publishing articles calling the revolt a "US-backed destabilization" and an "American-sponsored coup d'etat" and making false claims that the Ukrainian government replaced regional leaders with radicals from the Right Sector paramilitary group.[10]

[…]

Terminology Makes Its Way into Mainstream Media

The mainstream Western press paid little attention to the events in Kyiv until violence broke out, and media outlets were sent scrambling to find experts to help frame the revolution as it neared its dramatic climax in mid-February 2014. By then, the shear volume of Russian media reports outweighed those by Western reporters, and the Russian terminology began making its way into the US and European press. As European and American press tried to respond to growing interest, mysterious "experts" appeared with bylines in prominent Western media. With editorials headlines such as, "Rein in Ukraine's neo-fascists" and "Ukraine: far-right extremists at core of 'democracy' protest," alarmist reports about the role of far-right groups helped feed the Russian narrative (Speedie 2014, Walker 2014, Whelan 2014).

When war broke out in the Donbas region of Ukraine in spring 2014, RT and other media outlets were steadfast in framing the conflict as a fight between the new "fascist" leaders of the Ukrainian "junta" and local separatists in the east. Reports from Russian media—and what seems to have been general confusion on the part of the Western press—led major news networks to label the leaders of the armed conflict "pro-Russian rebels" or "pro-Russian separatists," despite the fact that many of them, including Igor Girkin—one of the chief architects of the early conflict—were actually Russian citizens.

In one *New York Times* report titled, "In Ukraine War, Kremlin Leaves No Fingerprints," the reporter interviews Girkin at length (also known as Strelkov) as well as the then-leader of the Donetsk People's Republic, Alexander Borodai, both of whom were born in Russia and came to Ukraine specifically to fight in the war. Girkin even had a background in Russian intelligence (Tavernise 2014). This report underscored the international press' inability to call the Kremlin on its insistence that it was not involved in the war.

In retrospect, it is puzzling that Russian fighters could be labelled rebels or separatists while participating in a conflict on foreign soil, but the influence of Russian media and the interest of the Western press to appear balanced and objective seem to have informed the choice of words during the early stages of the conflict. As late as July 2014, reports still appeared in major American news outlets claiming that "pro-Russian rebels" had seized Crimea, even though it was by then widely known that they were in fact Russian special forces. Even RT had by this time reported Putin saying in his own words that it was Russian soldiers who were the unmarked "little green men" who seized Ukrainian military bases in February-March 2014.

[…]

Applied Disinformation: Fake News to Confuse

In the confusion and fast-moving events of that spring, foreign reporters scrambled to figure out what was happening and to investigate the growing number of intriguing and scandalous stories coming from Russian media outlets. Russian television was at the forefront of the most extraordinary reports coming from the Donbas region. In one story, reported by Russia's First Channel, a woman claimed Ukrainian soldiers had crucified a young boy in the main square of the town of Slovyansk after pushing back separatist fighters—a report that prompted outrage in Russia and was then repeated on a number of alternative and pro-Russian English-language websites.[11,12] It wasn't until a reporter from Russian independent newspaper *Novaya Gazeta* was able to reach the village and investigate that the story was proven false. (Nemtsova 2014, Collison 2014). Another persistent feature of Russian media reports in 2014 was a woman named Maria Tsypko, who appeared in numerous Russian television reports as a victim of the Trade Union building fire in Odesa, as "Maria Vykina," the director of a charitable foundation in Donetsk, as a Donetsk lawyer, and as a referendum coordinator in Moscow (Kortunova 2014)[13].

These stories would be repeated on countless "news" websites that popped up seemingly overnight. Suspicious sites such as the "Kharkov News Agency" (new defunct) republished fake Russian reports and rumors about the Ukraine conflict. It turned out to have been bought by a Russian-based agency located at 55 Savushkina St. in St. Petersburg, the same address that was home to the Internet Research Agency, an agency known for housing paid internet trolls (Hamdan 2014, Chen 2015). Sites and YouTube accounts mimicking Ukrainian news portals, such as several fake Ukraine Today accounts, repeated fake stories and repeated Kremlin talking points.[14] This was not a new strategy, however. When residents of Ingushetiya, a federal district of southern Russia, used a site, ingushetiya.ru, to protest Russian policies toward local leaders in 2008, another site mimicking the local one, ingushetiyaru. net, appeared online to display pro-Kremlin talking points and to discredit the official protest site (Lysenko & Desouza 2010). This phenomenon has been observed recently in Latvia, where researchers tracked the appearance of fake news websites that appeared recently and began engaging in a large amount of activity targeting Latvians (Public Broadcasting of Latvia 2016).

[…]

While the seemingly endless stream of outrageous theories provided Ukrainian and Western bloggers with some much-needed levity after months of tragedy and war, the reports also marked what would be a turning point in the news coverage of the Russia-Ukraine war. Russian state media had fully exposed itself to Western journalists for what it was—a relentless source of disinformation that could not be reasoned with. It also showed a deeply cynical attitude toward newsgathering generally. While more straightforward propaganda is content to bash the audience over the head with one version and one narrative of an event, the 21st century Russian approach was more subtle. Instead of a single voice and a single interpretation, it created several, if not dozens of competing theories. Instead of trying to discredit the version initially reported responsibly in Western and Ukrainian media, it presented the many conspiracy theories as equally plausible in an attempt to sow confusion rather than certainty.

By discrediting the institution of journalism, no theory was more credible than another. It didn't matter who was right. In the minds of the ideal audience, no one was right and no one could be trusted. Since the outbreak of protests in Kyiv in 2013, Russian media had set out on a zero-sum game with the West and the international press to further erode trust in a news media industry already facing serious challenges at home. But by the time Western news outlets distanced themselves in earnest from their Russian colleagues and began to rely more on their own reporters, the war had been raging for more than three months, and Kremlin media had already left its mark on the narrative perpetuated both in the region and outside Eastern Europe.

By giving legitimacy to Russia's repeated denials of military involvement in Ukraine and by creating distractions for the Western press, Russian media was able to help the Kremlin distance itself from its actions and maintain plausible deniability in the eyes of an international audience. Paula Chertok argues that even the term "Ukraine crisis" rather than "war" created "a kind of distance from the reality of war's violence" (Chertok 2016). By reporting fake news, such as the crucifixion story, journalists who could have otherwise been reporting on the actual violence taking place in the Donbas were sent on wild-goose chases to debunk nonsense reports. It takes much more time and resources to disprove a fake story than it does to make one up. Russian media was able to stay a step ahead of responsible journalists—maintaining a steady barrage of fake and semi-truthful reports that would keep journalists in Ukraine and abroad distracted and bring a confusing haze to de-legitimize the media.

While Western, Ukrainian, and even many Russian journalists deserve praise for the courage they demonstrated in reporting the events of war and for seeking the truth in a messy situation, the news media industry was unable to fully see through the fog of disinformation in 2014. By presenting conspiracy theories, lies, and Kremlin denials with the same weight as real reporting based on fact-gathering and professional observation, major news outlets fell short of their duty to responsibly convey the events unfolding in Ukraine for the sake of an attempt to appear balanced and objective. It is a fool's errand to give responsible reporting the same benefit of the doubt and reverence as stories from questionable sources based on flimsy or no evidence. Russian propaganda in that sense was successful at exploiting the Western press and its commitment to investigation.

[…]

Notes

[1] Government of Russia 2000, pp. 9

[2] Clover, pp. 274

[3] Kramer, Andrew E. "Ukrainian Hackers Release Emails Tying Top Russian Official to Uprising." The New York Times. 27 October 2016. Available: https://www.nytimes.com/2016/10/28/world/europe/ukraine-russiaemails.html?_r=0

[4] Vladislav Surkov's leaked emails and their significance are discussed later in this paper in the "Gray Cardinal" section.

[5] Clover, pp. 269-271

[6] Darczewska, Jolanta. "The Anatomy of Russian Information Warfare: The Crimea Operation, A Case Study." Point of View. Centre for Eastern Studies. Warsaw, May 2014.

[7] 9 See Heickero paper on emerging cyber threats for an in-depth analysis of the ways Russia has used nonstate actors, including cyber criminals, to execute its cyberwarfare strategy.

[8] Dugin, Aleksandr. "Pravila polemiki s Vnutrennim Vragom: Nekotorye pravila polemiki v Novoy Rossii (posle Kryma)." Yevraziyskiy Soyuz Molodezhi. 11 March 2014. Available: http://rossia3.ru/politics/russia/vrag_polemika

[9] 8 Jared Taylor on RT: https://www.youtube.com/watch?v=eVgiiA-UP9Y and: https://www.youtube.com/watch?v=FLhK8LzT2Rg

[10] Hudson, Michael. "The New Cold War's Ukraine Gambit." Truthdig. 23 October 2014. Available: http://www.truthdig.com/report/item/the_new_cold_wars_ukraine_gambit_20141023

See also: Pfaff, William. "What Ukraine Really Needs." Truthdig. 13 May 2014. Available: http://www.truthdig.com/report/item/what_ukraine_really_needs_20140513

[11] Video preserved on YouTube: https://www.youtube.com/watch?v=Xf8Gt2Wnv74

[12] Some of these reports are still online, for example: https://slavyangrad.org/2014/07/13/slavyansk-refugee-remembers-brutal-execution/

[13] "Odesskaya gastrolersha rasszkazala o "publichnoy kazni" v Kramatorske." 10 August 2014.

"Odesskaya tragedia: ekspertiza ostavlyaet bol'she voprosov, chem otvetov." Novosti iz Rossii. 21 June 2014. Available: https://www.youtube.com/watch?v=pT6hwBnknJ8

"Maria - zhenskoe litso Novorossii." Sende Roche. 7 December 2014. Available: https://www.youtube.com/watch?v=x4jWXVQ-JOg

[14] Ukraine Today [fake account]. YouTube account. Available: https://www.youtube.com/channel/UCBnVFETAttP2-WuJPFM0mCw/about

4

A Case Study in Finding an Online Army

Tatiana Stanovaya

Tatyana Stanovaya is a political analyst who writes for the Institute of Modern Russia, a New York-based think tank.

The Nashi Movement was founded as a pro-government youth group, not unlike the Soviet-era Young Pioneers. Originally conceived as a way to police political protest, this model soon felt antiquated in a media environment that was at least somewhat committed to maintaining the appearance of a liberal democracy. In tracing the Nashi Movement's inability to find a place to openly articulate pro-government propaganda, its eventual move to the internet during the 2012 elections is symbolic of the greater investment Putin and other Kremlin figures put into the semi-discreet manipulation that the web brigades represented.

The Nashi ("Ours") movement appeared in 2005 along with other youth organizations that "worked" for the Kremlin. Nashi played a key role: it was a mass movement with a complicated but clearly defined structure, generous financing (mostly from the pockets of loyal oligarchs,) and access to top government officials. Its objective was to oppose a hypothetical "color revolution" in Russia that the Kremlin began to fear after the events in Georgia and Ukraine. The presidential administration received an order to be operationally ready in case of political destabilization. Many

"The Fate of the Nashi Movement: Where Will the Kremlin's Youth Go?" by Tatiana Stanovaya, The Institute of Modern Russia, Inc., March 26, 2013. Reprinted by permission.

in the Kremlin were convinced that the main risks originated not from inside, but from outside the country. That was when Putin's anti-Americanism began to emerge. "Color revolutions" in the post-Soviet space were a milestone in Russian-American relations: in Moscow's view, Washington used the "orange techniques" of manipulating and mobilizing street protests to encourage regime change.

The Kremlin had certainly overestimated both the outside influence and the internal political risks. At that moment, the conditions in Russia for a "Ukrainian scenario" did not exist. The regime's "vertical of power" had just been created, Putin's standings in the poll were never higher, and the ruling party, United Russia, was expecting to keep its two-thirds majority in the parliamentary elections. The opposition had been, for the most part, "purged," and, besides United Russia, the only other parliamentary parties were (and still are) docile groupings, all too willing to cooperate with the Kremlin rather than risk their seats in the State Duma.

Even at the time of its creation, the Nashi movement seemed superfluous. Nashi emerged from the pro-Putin group "Walking Together" that was headed by Vasily Yakemenko, who later became the connecting link between the movement and Deputy Kremlin Chief-of-Staff Vladislav Surkov. This marked the beginning of this project, the history of which can be divided roughly into four stages.

The first stage, which proved to be the most successful one, covers the period from 2005 to 2007. The movement declared its objective of "forcibly preserving" the current political system, with a gradual replacement of the ruling bureaucracy. (This last point was stated more for PR purposes than as a realistic goal). Liberals and "fascists" were defined as the main "targets" (in fact, they were equated with each other,) meaning all those who intended to "go into the streets" in order to influence the government in the way protesters did in Georgia and Ukraine. The Nashi movement was to become an alternative, aggressive street force ready to use tough methods against "destructive" elements. In an effort to attract the apolitical youth, the Kremlin offered as "bait" promises of a fast career path, access to top government officials, and participation in prestigious projects. "Commissars," who were at the head of the movement, would hold periodic meetings with the president and government ministers. Each year, Nashi organized a summer camp at Lake Seliger in the Tver region. As the movement's activists themselves wrote, Nashi was a "training system for professional managers to replace the current ruling elite."

However, the plan did not work out. United Russia was in no hurry to include young people from the Nashi movement in their election lists. The movement quickly became a mechanism for receiving financial resources through semi-official channels. Only a few members managed to obtain a promotion, and, even then, only with Surkov's personal patronage. Very soon, the movement became engulfed in scandals linked to its provocative actions against foreign ambassadors and Russian civic activists, as well as its use of "dirty tricks" to discredit political opponents. However, the first two years of Nashi's existence can be called its golden age. Businessmen, ministers, and United Russia members, who vocally "supported" Nashi's ambitious projects, "voluntarily" met with the movement's representatives.

The second stage began in late 2007 and lasted until approximately 2009. It was a period of political uncertainty for the movement. Dmitri Medvedev, who succeeded Putin as president, quickly distanced himself from Nashi. It was rumored that Medvedev's relationship with Surkov was difficult (later, it considerably improved,) and the new president, who passed for a "liberal," did not want to "soil himself" by association with a pro-Kremlin project of questionable reputation. During the 2008 presidential campaign, Nashi were pushed aside, the movement's financing decreased, and there was talk about closing down the project altogether.

However, the movement continued to be maintained, as they say, "just in case." The activities on Lake Seliger and provocative actions against the opposition continued. But the movement's participation in domestic politics declined—until the third stage in Nashi's history. As Surkov was drawing closer to Medvedev (which, in the end, cost him his post as deputy chief-of-staff), the Kremlin was trying to breathe new life into Nashi. In 2009 and 2010, many believed that President Medvedev would have a second term. The new agenda associated with a political "thaw," "liberal" rhetoric, a warming of relations with the US, and the encouragement of innovation demanded new ideas from the movement. It was not a coincidence that Nashi started showing an active interest in modernization. The Kremlin made an attempt at reforming the movement in order to include it into what it believed would be the new political reality and make it into President Medvedev's youth support base.

However, not much came out of it. Nashi have not become innovators, and their involvement in a number of scandals brought the government more harm than good. Suspicions about Nashi overseer Vasily Yakemenko's involvement in beating up well-known journalist Oleg Kashin became a turning-point. Despite Medvedev's promise to give this case special attention, the crime remains unsolved to this day. Clashes have also started to take place within the Kremlin: tensions arose between Medvedev's public relations team and Surkov over Nashi's harassment campaign against columnist Alexander Podrabinek. The pretext for the harassment was Podrabinek's op-ed in the online *Daily Journal*, in which he sharply criticized the Moscow Veterans Council for opposing the existence of a restaurant called "Anti-Soviet." The Presidential Human Rights Council and the president's press secretary, Natalya Timakova, stood up for the columnist, who was subjected to unprecedented pressure. Surkov, on the other hand, all but approved of Nashi's actions. For this and other reasons, Ella Pamfilova resigned as head of the Human Rights Council. Finally, members of Nashi were caught faking photographs that falsely portrayed Nashi as helping to put out wild fires that affected much of Russia in the summer of 2010. Sensationalist PR became the movement's "calling card."

However, it was neither the bad reputation nor the provocations that brought Medvedev's "romance" with Nashi to an end. Instead, it was the result of Prime Minister Vladimir Putin's decision to return to the Kremlin, which he announced during the now-famous United Russia congress in September 2011. This congress marked the political death of Medvedev, his agenda, his team and everything that it had achieved. Medvedev also "dragged down" Surkov, who was moved to the post of deputy prime minister for modernization, which Putin considered politically safe (the post of deputy prime minister for "nothing," as observers joked at the time). The scope of innovation was reduced to the Skolkovo project, which would soon be embroiled in criminal cases and investigations of embezzlement of budget funds.

The current stage in Nashi's existence began when Vyacheslav Volodin replaced Surkov in the Kremlin. Volodin considered the movement dangerous and was not inclined to continue pampering it. The current first deputy Kremlin chief-of-staff comes from the ruling party, and he disliked Surkov's attempts to force United Russia to include Nashi members on the party's election lists, especially since United Russia had its own youth division that competed with Nashi. It is no surprise that, after having dealt with the opposition, Volodin turned his attention to the legacy left to him by his predecessor.

According to *Vedomosti* newspaper, the Kremlin wants to reform the Nashi movement by changing its name and objectives. "We will not divide our young people into 'ours' and 'not ours,' there will not be such a word in the new name," assures *Vedomosti*'s source. Most likely, the word "commissar" will not be used either, though most of the movement's activists—the community of Nashi commissars—will stay. In place of the existing movement, there will be a project-oriented organization, where specific undertakings, decided on a competitive basis, will be supervised by specific managers. These projects will be of a nonpolitical social nature. The winners of competitions will receive both federal aid (in the form of presidential grants) and regional support. The current projects will be removed from the movement and entrusted to separate NGOs. According to the Kremlin, the project "Khryusha Against," aimed at consumer rights protection, is the most promising of all[1]. Other projects include "Stop boor," aimed at ending traffic violations, and the pro-fitness movement "Follow me." Internet projects that used to be managed by Nashi will become separate entities under the auspices of a foundation run by former Nashi spokesperson Kristina Potupchik. Kremlin sources are promising that these NGOs will become partners of the restructured movement.

In reality, however, this reform means the liquidation of Surkov's structure and the creation of a new organization loyal to Volodin. There will, no doubt, be a rotation of personnel that will bring new people into key positions. None of this means that the new movement will abandon the old tactics of provocation—this function could be fulfilled by the same NGOs, which have already appeared at opposition rallies with the aim of discrediting them.

Despite the fact that the Kremlin's youth policy has not changed, Volodin does not need the Nashi movement in its present form. The Russian government is still "keeping in mind" the possibility of a "color revolution," especially in the context of a growing protest activity and a maturing opposition. The political situation in Russia is becoming less predictable, and the risks of destabilization are growing. The regime is undergoing a moral crisis and is increasingly vulnerable against a background of anticorruption exposés by civic activists.

Under such circumstances, the tactics employed by Kremlin-mobilized forces at demonstrations will become increasingly rougher and more confrontational. The reformed Nashi movement will lose its key role, and more conservative elements such as "Orthodox" activists, public organizations like Sergey Kurginyan's All-Russia Parents Assembly, and even the Cossacks will move to the forefront. The belligerent support for Putin from marginal groups is becoming more ideological and aggressive toward the opposition in general, and liberals in particular. It may very well be that these new tactics will make us nostalgic for the times when the relatively innocuous Nashi were marching in the streets.

Notes

1 Khryusha is known to virtually every Russian as a piglet in the bedtime television program, "Good Night Little Ones," watched for generations by young children and their parents. The closest American equivalent would be Big Bird.

5

A Case Study in Using an Online Army

Miriam Elder

Miriam Elder is an American journalist who wrote for the Guardian's *Moscow office before becoming the world editor for* Buzzfeed.

Emails released by a group allegedly affiliated with the international hacktivist group Anonymous revealed that Nashi paid bloggers to overwhelm negative coverage of Putin. They accomplished this by making hundreds of comments, hitting the "dislike" button for anti-Putin coverage on platforms like YouTube, and organizing pro-Putin groups on the internet. While merely a small scandal at the time, the Nashi incident indicated the expanding reach of propaganda, suggesting it would go beyond the message boards of the last decade and burrow itself into the social media platforms that still dominate discourse today.

A pro-Kremlin group runs a network of internet trolls, seeks to buy flattering coverage of Vladimir Putin and hatches plans to discredit opposition activists and media, according to private emails allegedly hacked by a group calling itself the Russian arm of Anonymous.

The group has uploaded hundreds of emails it says are to, from and between Vasily Yakemenko, the first leader of the youth group Nashi – now head of the Kremlin's Federal Youth Agency – its spokeswoman, Kristina Potupchik, and other activists. The emails detail payments to journalists and bloggers, the group alleges.

"Polishing Putin: hacked emails suggest dirty tricks by Russian youth group," by Miriam Elder, Guardian News and Media Limited, February 7, 2012. Reprinted by permission.

Potupchik declined to confirm or deny the veracity of the emails, but appeared to acknowledge that her email had been hacked. "I will not comment on illegal actions," she told the *Guardian*.

Nikita Borovikov, the current leader of Nashi, said: "For several years, I've got used to the fact that our email is periodically hacked. When I heard the rumours that it had been hacked, I wasn't shocked, and have paid no attention to this problem. I'm a law-abiding person, and have nothing to fear of hiding, so I pay no attention."

Apparently sent between November 2010 and December 2011, the emails appear to confirm critics' longstanding suspicions that the group uses sinister methods, funded by the Kremlin, to attack perceived enemies and pay for favourable reports while claiming that Putin's popularity is unassailable.

They provide particular insight into the group's strategy to boost pro-Putin coverage on the internet, which in contrast to television is seen as being ruled by the opposition. Several emails sent from activists to Potupchik include price lists for pro-Putin bloggers and commenters, indicating that some are paid as much as 600,000 roubles (£12,694) for leaving hundreds of comments on negative press articles on the internet. One email, sent to Potupchik on 23 June 2011, suggests that the group planned to spend more than R10m to buy a series of articles about its annual Seliger summer camp in two popular Russian tabloids, Moskovsky Komsomolets and Komsomolskaya Pravda, and the daily Nezavisimaya Gazeta. Arkady Khantsevich, deputy editor of Nezavisimaya Gazeta, denied that his journalists accepted money for articles, a widespread practice in post-Soviet Russia.

"Yes, we wrote about Seliger, and will continue to," he said. "But the paper has never entered into a financial contract, including with political parties." He added that the journalist who covered the summer camp had written under a pseudonym, and the newspaper would not be investigating the claim.

A spokesman for Moskovsky Komsomolets's press service declined to comment: "I don't read what they write on the internet about MK being paid for stories about Seliger. It doesn't interest us." Komsomolskaya Pravda has not responded publicly and could not be reached for comment.

The leak comes as Putin faces the greatest challenge to his rule since first coming to power 12 years ago, with mass street demonstrations building momentum before a presidential vote on 4 March that is expected to return him to the presidency after a four-year interlude as prime minister.

Nashi was created precisely to stand up to any such challenge to Putin's rule. It was formed in 2005 after pro-democracy revolutions in neighbouring Ukraine and Georgia. Thousands of Nashi activists, mostly bussed into the Russian capital from neighbouring provinces, took to the streets in December as Russia's protest movement took hold after a contested parliamentary vote.

The Kremlin has been looking beyond the youth movement lately. On Saturday, the day of the latest opposition protest, the Kremlin turned out thousands of people at a rally in support of Putin's candidacy. Despite the fact that Putin remains Russia's most popular politician, reports were widespread that many of those demonstrating in his support had been forced by employers or paid to take part, echoing the picture painted in the emails of a regime determined to keep up the appearance of his popularity.

"These strategies – what they do on the internet and how they gather protests – are very similar," said Alexey Navalny, the anti-corruption blogger who is helping to lead the protest movement. "Their main problem is that they don't have real people who are ready to say something in support of them. They don't have one person who supports them for free. So they pay."

According to the emails, Nashi manipulates YouTube viewcounts and ratings, calling on paid Nashi activists to "dislike" anti-regime videos.

The emails show the particular attention Nashi pays to Navalny, whose anti-corruption blog and Twitter account have been instrumental in organising anti-Putin sentiment. Activists are seen proposing various ideas to Yakemenko – from projects that came to fruition, such as a cartoon video comparing Navalny to Hitler – to others that were rejected, including a suggestion that someone dress up like the blogger to beg for alms in front of the US embassy. Putin and his supporters continue to insist that opposition protests have been funded and provoked by the west.

The correspondence goes some way towards explaining the apparent paranoia, showing how Nashi, curated by Yakemenko and his recently deposed boss, the Kremlin ideologue Vladislav Surkov, spends huge sums of money to create the illusion of Putin's unfailing popularity.

It appears to confirm that a host of pro-Putin stunts advertised as spontaneous acts by average citizens were in fact orchestrated by Nashi. Among these are a web-based group called I Really Do Like Putin and the all-female Putin's Army, which became notorious last summer after hosting a car wash in support of Putin and calling on women around the country to tear their shirts off for the leader.

Speculation that Nashi is behind pro-Putin stunts, pays internet commenters to troll anti-regime sites and orders DDoS (distributed denial of service) attacks have long swirled around. But the emails, if confirmed, would provide an unprecedented look into the system's inner workings.

The Anonymous hackers told the online news portal Gazeta. ru, in an interview published late on Monday that they carried out the hack, planned since spring of last year, "as a sign of protest against the government's actions in the public internet sphere". "Our ultimate goal is to not allow bandits to bring the Russian internet to its knees," the group said.

The Russian government has so far avoided cracking down on internet freedoms, and both Putin and the current president, Dmitry Medvedev, have spoken out against internet censorship. Yet activists have long complained of co-ordinated attacks that have brought down websites or flooded commentary with pro-Putin spam. Several liberal websites, including those of the radio station Ekho Moskvy and the election monitoring group Golos, were brought down by DDoS attacks on the eve of the country's 4 December parliamentary vote.

"Everything that has been published, we already know," Navalny said. "[Nashi] undertake the organisation of provocative actions, both physically and on the internet."

Opposition leaders have also accused Nashi of being behind a series of attacks including repeated scuffles with the liberal youth leader Ilya Yashin and an incident in which ammonia-laced cola was thrown in the face of the former deputy prime minister Boris Nemtsov. Nashi denied being involved in the latter.

As British-Russian relations spiralled towards a low in 2006, the group launched a campaign of harassment against the former UK ambassador Tony Brenton after he met opposition groups. It has since turned its attention to the internet, analysts say.

The emails suggest a palpable concern within Nashi and the Kremlin after Russia's contested parliamentary vote on 4 December launched an unexpected protest movement that brought thousands on to the streets of Moscow for the first time. Activists write to Yakemenko proposing various "provocative actions" designed to discredit the quickly growing movement.

On 11 December, one day after up to 50,000 people gathered on Bolotnaya Square in an unprecedented show of discontent with Putin, Borovikov writes to Yakemenko to propose different means of dealing with the opposition. "If we don't do this all in time, these public opinion leaders will continue to protest on the streets and all this will turn into a Ukrainian Maidan," Borovikov writes, referring to the square in Kiev that hosted Ukraine's pro-democracy, "orange revolution".

Asked by the *Guardian* about the hack, Borovikov said: "I'm not ready to discuss any provocations. It's not correct to discuss this in principle. Unfortunately, it has become part of life to get into personal things, but it is not very nice to discuss it. It's amoral. To think Nashi, as a social youth organisation, has a lot of money is a delusion. The main resource of any social organisation is its people: people's time, people's efforts."

Yakemenko's office directed all queries to Potupchik, who did not answer subsequent requests for comment.

Revealing rumours long taken as fact, the emails are unlikely to have an effect on the opposition's methods or goals. Borovikov's alleged words may turn out to be prescient. "Either the powers fulfil our legal demands or people will turn out and refuse to leave," Navalny said.

Most of the leaked emails are brief and discuss the practicality of orchestrating the pro-Putin work that Nashi feeds on. One email provides a rare glimpse into a top activist's thinking, as Potupchik emails several Nashi leaders, known, in the group's lingo as commisars, to speak highly of Yakemenko.

"If someone thinks that they can be on my team and not play by my rules, they can leave," Potupchik, well known for her colourful language, allegedly wrote on 26 October 2011.

"If you think that in this country another person can be found who would create such a structure, who would drag into this work all the dregs of the provincial towns, who would make provincial sh*ts into princesses of the capital, then f*ck off. Maybe you're not happy with something. Maybe you're not paid that much, you don't like how you're treated, don't like your office, or your work schedule."

"I ask you not to bother me and to leave this horrible work."

6

Templates and Guidelines for Russian Trolls

Aric Toler

Aric Toler holds a master's degree in Slavic languages and literature from the University of Kansas.

Through looking at documents and interviews collected by Andrei Soshnikov for the St. Petersburg publication Moi Region, *Toler explains the details of how Russian troll factories operate. The evidence presented includes guidelines for posting by the Internet Research Agency (IRA), examples of sock puppet accounts and their online activity, and excerpts from interviews with insiders and experts. The viewpoint also points out that some—such as Ukrainian officials—are attempting to combat Russian trolls with their own web brigades.*

It has long been an open secret that an army of paid Russian Internet commenters works out of a sleepy residential neighborhood in northern St. Petersburg. A new report from *Moi Region* and *Novaya Gazeta* provides an even more revealing view into the so-called "troll den" that allegedly produces thousands of pro-Kremlin posts and comments every day.

Andrei Soshnikov of the weekly St. Petersburg publication *Moi Region* secured a collection of documents and an interview from a former employee of the notorious Internet Research Agency, which employs over 400 people in a non-descript building located at 55 Savushkina str. in St. Petersburg.

The interview mostly confirms what many already know about the hundreds of employees who collectively manage thousand of social media accounts on LiveJournal, Twitter, and other platforms. These users produce pro-Kremlin posts, based on prepackaged talking points, and sandwich them between apolitical posts about photography, fashion, sports, and other trivial subjects. Aside from a rare, albeit brief, undercover video of the Internet commenters at work, the most interesting part of Soshnikov's article is a revealing cache of documents that provides a partial list of LiveJournal accounts operated by employees, along with the talking points provided to employees following the assassination of opposition leader Boris Nemtsov.

Working as a paid commenter is not as easy as one might think, as the Internet Research Agency has strict and demanding guidelines for fabricated posts.

General requirements for writing posts:

– MANDATORY use of keywords in the post's headline (the prioritized keywords are highlighted in bold in this technical specification),

– MANDATORY use of keywords in the body of the post,

– MANDATORY use of graphics/images or videos found on YouTube on the subject of the post (using the images done by the Creative Department is highly welcome)

– A post must contain no less than 700 characters for those working the day shift, and no less than 1000 for those working the night shift.

If a post is non-compliant with the points above, it will not be counted.

Along with these general guidelines, specific talking points and keywords for various subjects—Ukraine, the E.U., the United States, the Russian opposition, etc.—are regularly distributed to the busy staff. The list of "troll"-operated LiveJournal accounts that Soshnikov provides confirms his article's findings and reveals countless posts that conform to these guidelines.

A typical "sock puppet" account is operated by "Natalya Drozdova," who has a LiveJournal blog, a Twitter account, a Facebook page, a Google+ profile, and a VK account. Of course, Natalya Drozdova is not real—the accounts are operated by an employee named Tatyana Kazakbayeva, according to Soshnikov's documents—but "she" is interested in "art, psychology, and all that happens in the world." Most of Natalya's posts are unremarkable, such as a post about Facebook removing the "feeling fat" status, a whole array of Fifty Shades of Grey parodies, and a post requesting advice after a bizarre conflict with a shopping mall janitor over bringing a baby carriage into the bathroom.

But Natalya also has strong opinions on allowing Iran to continue its nuclear program and wonders out loud if the Russian opposition movement murdered Boris Nemtsov as a "sacrifice" to further its own ends. The musings of "Natalya Drozdova" follow the guidelines set out by the Internet Research Agency on February 28, the same day as her post on Nemtsov was published.

Leaked brief from February 28:

Technical brief from February 28: "Main idea: Form an opinion that Ukrainian officials could be involved in the death of the Russian opposition figure. [...] Nemtsov's death was not accidental given the conditions of achieving the Minsk accords and possible improvement of cooperation between Ukraine and Russia. Now Russia has once again become the country that the West reacts negatively towards. This is an obvious provocation, aimed at rousing dissatisfaction from the members of the opposition, who will now begin calling for marches and rallies to overthrow the government."

"Natalya"'s LiveJournal post on Feb 28:

Since morning I've been sitting and reading about the circumstances of Nemtsov's death. The further I read the more I am convinced: he was simply sacrificed by his own people. Where he was killed (near the Kremlin walls), who he was with at the time (a model from Kiev, Anna Duritskaya), how he was killed (not a simple car or plane crash, but a bullet wound), and also the fact that the girl herself, regardless of many fired shots, was unharmed, point to it being a provocation. Done to provoke people to go out into the streets and make a revolution in our country (how that would end is a separate conversation).

RuNet expert Anton Nossik, in his comment on the *Moi Region* story, notes that not all pro-Kremlin comments are paid for, but the fabricated ones are clearly visible, and that means paid trolls have little effect on the audience's political views.

Certainly, not all pro-government comments on the Internet are paid for. Among the RuNet's 70 million users there are millions who rejoice about the war in Ukraine, for instance. Their posts and comments reek of ill health, of inferiority, of rage... But in the posts composed based on talking points a living human is hard to see.

The propaganda war online has received almost as much press as the real conflict in eastern Ukraine, and Russia seems to possess greater resources on both fronts. Ukraine has recently tried to match the Russian troll army by recruiting its own brigade of Internet commenters to "fight propaganda with facts and evidence." However, as this new glimpse into the front lines of the online information war shows, the Russian side is greater in size, well-funded, and more disciplined in its construction of a massive echo chamber on the RuNet.

7

Today's Troll Armies

Paul Gallagher

Paul Gallagher is a reporter for the Independent, *a national newspaper in the UK.*

Three years after emails revealed a network of bloggers being paid by a shadowy youth organization, Marat Burkhard revealed the day-to-day operations inside the much more centralized form that Russia's web brigades had taken: the Internet Research Agency (IRA). Employing full-time staffs in major cities like St. Petersburg, IRA employees would be given talking points to push and quotas of how many comments they would have to post about them. Sometimes this would involve creating entirely fictional debates on social media platforms: one employee voicing a deliberately illogical anti-Putin opinion in order to be silenced by a small army of them in the next room.

They are the online army of pro-Kremlin commentators familiar to anyone who dares read below the line on web articles about Russia.

Now one former foot soldier has broken ranks to expose the Orwellian 'troll factories' where state-sponsored employees work 12-hour shifts posting pro-Putin propaganda on news and social media websites.

St Petersburg blogger Marat Burkhard lifted the lid on the 24/7 life in an unassuming four-storey modern building he

"Revealed: Putin's army of pro-Kremlin bloggers," by Paul Gallagher, independent.co.uk, March 27, 2015. Reprinted by permission.

compared to the Ministry of Truth from George Orwell's *1984*. Hundreds of workers are paid above-average salaries of around £500 a month and required to write at least 135 comments per day - or face immediate dismissal. The repressive system's strict rules and regulations include no laughing and fines for being a minute late. Friendship is frowned upon.

Asked if he agreed it sounded like something from Orwell's dystopian classic novel Mr. Burkhard said: "Yes, that's right, the Ministry of Truth. You work in the Ministry of Truth, which is the Ministry of Lies, and everyone kind of believes in this truth. Yes, you're right, it's Orwell."

The structure is simple. Once a story has been published on a local news forum the troll army goes to work by dividing into teams of three: one plays the 'villain' criticising the authorities with the other two debate with him and support government officials. One of the pro-Kremlin pair needs to provide a graphic or image that fits in the context and the other posts a link to some content that supports his argument.

"You see? Villain, picture, link," Mr. Burkhard told Radio Free Europe/Radio Liberty. "So in this way our little threesome traverses the country, stopping at every forum, starting with Kaliningrad and ending in Vladivostok. We create the illusion of actual activity on these forums. We write something, we answer each other. There are keywords, tags, that are needed for search engines. We're given five keywords – for example 'defence minister' or 'Russian army'. All three of us have to make sure these keywords appear all over the place in our comments".

The funniest assignment he was given involved President Barack Obama chewing gum in India and spitting it out.

"[I was told] 'You need to write 135 comments about this, and don't be shy about how you express yourself. Write whatever you want, just stick the word Obama in there a lot and then cover it over with profanities'.

"In the assignment, there's always a conclusion you've got to make that Obama doesn't know anything about culture. You stick him in ancient India and he chews gum there. It's funny in the sense that they're ready to grab onto any little thing. On the other hand, it's not funny. It's absurd and it crosses a line."

There are teams dedicated to Facebook and other social media. "There are about 40 rooms with about 20 people sitting in each, and each person has their assignments. They write and write all day, and it's no laughing matter — you can get fired for laughing. And so every day, any news does the trick — it could be Obama, could be [German Chancellor Angela] Merkel, could be Greece, North Korea.

"Even a political scientist can't be an expert about the entire world, but here people are expected to write about everything. And how you write doesn't matter; you can praise or scold. You just have put those keywords in."

Staff are forbidden from leaving the building during their 12-hour day or night shifts which they work two days on two off. After two months Mr. Burkhard had had enough.

"I decided I can't engage in absurd work. It's all absurd. I don't share this ideology, I'm absolutely against it. I was located in the enemy camp. To keep on working made no sense, even for money, because it's such hard work that — just forget it, forget the money. Just don't make me go there anymore."

8

Russia's Troll Armies Attack Europe

Robert Booth, Matthew Weaver, Alex Hern, Stacee Smith, and Shaun Walker

Robert Booth, Matthew Weaver, Alex Hern, and Shaun Walker all write for the Guardian. *Stacee Smith is a freelance writer.*

In 2016, the UK voted by a narrow margin to leave the European Union. Many international observers saw the "Brexit" vote as a victory for Putin's Russia, which had long seen the EU as their primary geopolitical rival in Europe. A study of the media environment surrounding the vote discovered that the IRA ran over 400 accounts on Twitter intended to deliver pro-Brexit opinions, camouflaged as the opinions of outraged British voters. The study also discovered that the IRA had been involved in similar activities in other divisive European political debates, such as Catalan independence and the French general election. While not able to directly alter votes, these Twitter accounts often were able to inflame issues that might otherwise remain on the fringe of electoral culture.

Concern about Russian influence in British politics has intensified as it emerged that more than 400 fake Twitter accounts believed to be run from St Petersburg published posts about Brexit.

"Russia Used Hundreds Of Fake Accounts To Tweet About Brexit, Data Shows," by Robert Booth, Matthew Weaver, Alex Her, Stacee Smith, and Shaun Walker, Guardian News and Media Limited, November 14, 2017. Reprinted by permission.

Researchers at the University of Edinburgh identified 419 accounts operating from the Russian Internet Research Agency (IRA) attempting to influence UK politics out of 2,752 accounts suspended by Twitter in the US.

One of the accounts run from the Kremlin-linked operation attempted to stir anti-Islamic sentiment during the Westminster Bridge terror attack in March in a bogus post claiming a Muslim woman ignored victims – a claim that was highlighted by mainstream media outlets including Mail Online and the Sun.

For days after, the tweeter was gleefully sharing press clippings. "Wow … I'm on the Daily Mail front page! Thank you British libs! You're making me famous," he said, referring to an article that appeared on Mail Online and which still bore the tweet at the time of writing.

A day later, he tweeted: "I'm on The Sun! Thank you again, British libs! Now I'm even more famous!"

Damian Collins, the chairman of the Commons culture, media and sport select committee, which is investigating fake news, said the Russian agency appeared to be attempting to divide society and destabilise politics.

The Conservative MP wants Twitter to tell the committee how it believes Russia has been attempting to influence UK politics.

"What is at stake is whether Russia has constructed an architecture which means they have thousands of accounts with which they can bombard [us] with fake news and hyper-partisan content," he said.

"We need to understand how widespread it is and what the impact is on the democratic process."

Collins has demanded that Twitter's chief executive, Jack Dorsey, supply examples of posts from the Internet Research Agency about British politics – citing concern at possible "interference by foreign actors in the democratic process" of the UK.

"This is information they hold and I can't see any reason they should be delaying supplying it," he said.

The developments come after the US Congress intelligence committee investigated Russian troll campaigning in the US election of November 2016.

Twitter told the House committee that it had suspended 2,752 accounts which were tweeting about the US election because it believed they were controlled from Russia. The committee said it "may well be just the tip of the iceberg".

Hundreds of paid bloggers work round the clock at the IRA to flood Russian internet forums, social networks and the comments sections of western publications – sowing disinformation, praising the country's president, Vladimir Putin, and raging at the west.

The agency has been linked to a businessman who was once Putin's favourite chef.

Prof Laura Cram, director of neuropolitics research at the University of Edinburgh, told the *Guardian* that at least 419 of those accounts tweeted about Brexit a total of 3,468 times – mostly after the referendum had taken place.

Archives of the now deleted Russian accounts show they included people purporting to be a US Navy veteran, a Tennessee Republican and a Texan patriot – all tweeting in favour of Brexit.

Labour deputy leader Tom Watson urged Theresa May to "bring political pressure to bear on tech giants to reveal the extent to which their platforms have been hijacked, and to take action against agents of the Russian state who use their platforms to disseminate misinformation and untruths".

He said tech companies including Twitter and Facebook "haven't done enough to identify and weed out the fake profiles and automated content that pose a direct threat to our democracy".

On Monday, May gave a speech in which she said Russia's actions were "threatening the international order on which we all depend".

She accused Russia of meddling in elections and planting fake stories in the media to "weaponise information" and sow discord in the west.

Concerns about Russia's cyber-operations have also been raised elsewhere in Europe.

Spain's prime minister, Mariano Rajoy, claimed on Monday that half of the Twitter accounts that amplified the issue of Catalan independence were registered in Russia and 30% in Venezuela.

Others have voiced concerns that Russian social media accounts also sought to influence this year's French and German elections.

A spokesperson for Twitter said the company "recognises that the integrity of the election process itself is integral to the health of a democracy. As such, we will continue to support formal investigations by government authorities into election interference as required."

The Russian tweets identified by Twitter as coming from the IRA included one by an account holder using the name @SouthLoneStar.

He reportedly said: "I hope UK after #BrexitVote will start to clean their land from muslim invasion!" and "UK voted to leave future European Caliphate! #BrexitVote."

The same account posted a widely shared tweet at the time of the March terror attack on Westminster Bridge in London.

It posted a photograph of a woman in a headscarf passing the scene of the attack with the caption: "Muslim woman pays no mind to the terror attack, casually walks by a dying man while checking phone #PrayForLondon #Westminster #BanIslam."

The woman said later: "Not only have I been devastated by witnessing the aftermath of a shocking and numbing terror attack, I've also had to deal with the shock of finding my picture plastered all over social media by those who could not look beyond my attire, who draw conclusions based on hate and xenophobia."

Another suspended account appeared to be a Republican from Tennessee. @TEN_GOP quoted Nigel Farage telling Fox News about Brexit and Donald Trump: "What you've seen this year is just ordinary, decent people, the little people, who've said 'We've had enough. We want change.'"

@WadeHarriot, purporting to be a former member of the US Navy, retweeted criticisms of "leftists" for "trying to subvert #Brexit" and predictions of "#Brexit #Frexit #Grexit".

Cram said the content of the Brexit tweets overall was "quite chaotic and it seems to be aimed at wider disruption. There's not an absolutely clear thrust. We pick up a lot on refugees and immigration."

She stressed that more research is needed to establish the extent of the tweets' influence, and urged caution about drawing conclusions from the relatively small number of troll accounts so far identified. About 78% of the tweets came after the Brexit vote on 23 June 2016, she added.

Russia has been adamant it did not interfere in any way in the EU referendum. "We closely followed the voting but never interfered or sought to influence it," Putin said the day after the poll.

However, there is no doubt that many in Moscow welcomed the outcome. An EU without Britain would be less united on sanctions against Russia, many Russian officials hoped, because it would lose one of its stronger foreign policy voices and would be too consumed with its own internal problems to prioritise Russia policy.

At the time, the former US ambassador to Russia, Michael McFaul, said the vote to leave the EU was "a giant victory for Putin's foreign policy objectives".

The US Congressional investigation into Russian meddling through social media also gathered evidence from Facebook that between June 2015-August 2017 there were 470 accounts on the platform associated with the IRA and that 126 million Americans are likely to have seen content from an IRA page.

9

Russian Trolls on Facebook for Trump

House Permanent Select Committee on Intelligence

The United States House Permanent Select Committee on Intelligence was established in 1977 to replace the Select Committee on Intelligence, which had been established two years earlier to investigate illegal activities committed by the CIA and FBI. Twenty-two members of Congress are in the Committee and nine of them caucus with the Democratic Party, currently the minority party in Congress.

A 2018 memo released by the Democratic minority in the House's Permanent Select Committee on Intelligence quotes a recent indictment by the Department of Justice's Special Counsel Robert Mueller of thirteen Russian individuals and three Russian organizations, including the infamous IRA. Much of the alleged activity occurred on Facebook, where Russian agents purportedly bought at least 3,519 advertisements that were aimed at American voters, many of which betrayed "a clear preference for...Trump." The US constitution forbids anyone holding government office from receiving assistance from a foreign state, which is what has prompted an investigation to ascertain if any collusion between the Trump campaign and these Russian individuals and organizations occurred.

On February 16, 2018 Special Counsel Robert S. Mueller III indicted 13 Russian individuals and three Russian

"Facebook Ads Exposing Russia's Effort to Sow Discord Online: The Internet Research Agency and Advertisements," House Permanent Select Committee on Intelligence. Courtesy of the House Permanent Select Committee on Intelligence.

organizations for engaging in operations to interfere with U.S. political and electoral processes, including the 2016 presidential election. This was a significant step forward in exposing a surreptitious social media campaign and holding accountable those responsible for this attack. The indictment spells out in exhaustive detail the breadth and systematic nature of this conspiracy, dating back to 2014, as well as the multiple ways in which Russian actors misused online platforms to carry out their clandestine operations.

Throughout the indictment, Mueller lays out important facts about the activities of the Internet Research Agency (IRA)—the notorious Russian "troll" farm—and its operatives:

"Defendants, posing as U.S. persons and creating false U.S. personas, operated social media pages and groups designed to attract U.S. audiences. These groups and pages, which addressed divisive U.S. political and social issues, falsely claimed to be controlled by U.S. activists when, in fact, they were controlled by Defendants. Defendants also used the stolen identities of real U.S. persons to post on ORGANIZATION-controlled social media accounts. Over time, these social media accounts became Defendants' means to reach significant numbers of Americans for purposes of interfering with the U.S. political system, including the presidential election of 2016."

The indictment also notes that the IRA:

"[H]ad a strategic goal to sow discord in the U.S. political system, including the 2016 U.S. presidential election. Defendants posted derogatory information about a number of candidates, and by early to mid-2016, Defendants' operations included supporting the presidential campaign of then-candidate Donald J. Trump ("Trump Campaign") and disparaging Hillary Clinton. Defendants made various expenditures to carry out those activities, including buying political advertisements on social media in the names of U.S. persons and entities. Defendants also staged political rallies inside the United States, and while posing as U.S. grassroots entities and U.S. persons, and without revealing their Russian identities and ORGANIZATION affiliation, solicited and compensated real U.S. persons to promote or disparage candidates. Some

Defendants, posing as U.S. persons and without revealing their Russian association, communicated with unwitting individuals associated with the Trump Campaign and with other political activists to seek to coordinate political activities."

Additionally, in their October 2016 joint attribution statement, the Department of Homeland Security and the Office of the Director of National Intelligence laid out the Intelligence Community's assessment that senior Russian government officials had directed a hacking-and-dumping campaign to interfere in the November 2016 U.S. election. In its subsequent Intelligence Community Assessment (ICA) in January 2017, the Intelligence Community further documented Moscow's interference in our election and its efforts to assist Donald Trump's campaign and harm Hillary Clinton's.

According to the ICA:

"Russian President Vladimir Putin ordered an influence campaign in 2016 aimed at the US presidential election. Russia's goals were to undermine public faith in the US democratic process, denigrate Secretary Clinton, and harm her electability and potential presidency."

The ICA also assesses that:

"Putin and the Russian Government developed a clear preference for President-elect Trump."

Putin and the Russian government, the ICA explained:

"[A]spired to help President-elect Trump's election chances when possible by discrediting Secretary Clinton and publicly contrasting her unfavorably to him."

The tools to carry out this covert operation were multifaceted, according to the Assessment:

Moscow's influence campaign followed a Russian messaging strategy that blends covert intelligence operations—such as cyber activity—with overt efforts by Russian Government agencies, state-funded media, third-party intermediaries, and paid social media users or "trolls."

As explained in our Minority Views, the House Intelligence Committee Minority affirmed the ICA's findings following a review of extensive classified and unclassified evidence in the course of the investigation, including significant information discovered since the release of the ICA in January 2017.

The House Intelligence Committee Minority has worked to expose the Kremlin's exploitation of social media networks since the ICA was first published, highlighting this issue for the American public during an open hearing with social media companies in November 2017. The Committee Minority also released a list of Twitter accounts associated with the Internet Research Agency and a representative sampling of Facebook ads paid for by the group.

Throughout our investigation, the Committee Minority has sought to make available to the public advertisements, accounts and information related to the IRA because of our strong belief that sunlight is the best disinfectant against any future attempts to weaken our democracy or interfere in our free and fair elections process. Moreover, Congress does not have the technical expertise to fully analyze this data—that lies in outside groups such as news publications and academic researchers. We hope that the publication of these materials will facilitate this important work.

As Ranking Member Adam Schiff stated during the Committee's November 2017 open hearing with senior officials from Facebook, Twitter, and Google:

> *"[The Russian] social media campaign was designed to further a broader Kremlin objective: sowing discord in the U.S. by inflaming passions on a range of divisive issues. The Russians did so by weaving together fake accounts, pages, and communities to push politicized content and videos, and to mobilize real Americans to sign online petitions and join rallies and protests. Russia exploited real vulnerabilities that exist across online platforms and we must identify, expose, and defend ourselves against similar covert influence operations in the future. The companies here today must play a central role as we seek to better protect legitimate political expression, while preventing cyberspace from being misused by our adversaries."*

As part of that continuing effort to educate the public and seek additional analysis, the Committee Minority is making available all IRA advertisements identified by Facebook. This is an effort to be fully transparent with the public, allow outside experts to analyze the data, and provide the American people a fuller accounting of Russian efforts to sow discord and interfere in our democracy.

Facebook Data

As part of the Committee's open hearing with social media companies in November 2017, the Minority used a number of advertisements as exhibits, and made others available as part of a small representative sampling. During the hearing, Committee Members noted the breadth of activity by the IRA on Facebook:

- 3,393 advertisements purchased (a total 3,519 advertisements total were released after more were identified by the company);
- More than 11.4 million American users exposed to those advertisements;
- 470 IRA-created Facebook pages;
- 80,000 pieces of organic content created by those pages; and
- Exposure of organic content to more than 126 million Americans.

The Facebook advertisements we are publishing today have been carefully reviewed by the Committee Minority and redacted by Facebook to protect personally-identifiable information (PII). To protect innocent victims, Facebook—at the urging of the Committee Minority—also has notified users whose genuine online events were unwittingly promoted by the IRA.

The data made available today does not include the 80,000 pieces of organic content shared on Facebook by the IRA. We expect to make this content public in the future.

10

Troll Lives Matter? Russian Infiltration of the Black Lives Matter Movement

Micah White

Micah White is an American activist and was a co-creator of the Occupy Wall Street movement.

One American target of the IRA was the Black Lives Matter movement. They attempted to troll the movement via an IRA-run group called "Black Matters," which at one point boasted 200,000 likes on Facebook. In order to secure further legitimacy, they reached out to actual American activists like Micah White, who had became a national figure after his work with Occupy Wall Street. White writes about his experience with them, providing insight into both Russia's web brigades and how they figure into the long history of activists being used as pawns in cold wars between nations.

I have sometimes been approached by persons that I suspected were either agents or assets of intelligence agencies during the 20 years that I have been a social activist. The tempo of these disconcerting encounters increased when I abruptly relocated to a remote town on the Oregon coast after the defeat of Occupy Wall Street, a movement I helped lead. My physical inaccessibility seemed to provoke a kind of desperation among these shadowy forces.

"I Started Occupy Wall Street—Russia Tried to Co-Opt Me," by Micah White, November 2, 2017. Micah White is the co-creator of Occupy Wall Street and author of *The End of Protest: A New Playbook for Revolution.* Reprinted by permission.

There was the man purporting to be an internet repair technician who arrived unsolicited at our rural home and then tinkered with our modem. Something felt odd and I was not surprised when CNN later reported that posing as internet repairmen is a known tactic of the FBI.

I've had other suspicious encounters. A couple seeking advice on starting a spiritual activist community, for example, but whose story made little sense. And a former Occupy activist who moved to my town to, I felt, undermine my activism and gather information about me.

Those few friends that I confided in dismissed my suspicions as mild paranoia. And perhaps it was. I stopped talking about it and instead became highly selective about the people I met, emails I responded to and invitations I accepted.

I hinted at the situation by adding a section to my book, The End of Protest, warning activists to beware of frontgroups. And, above all, I learned to trust my intuition – if someone gave me a tingly sense then I stayed away. That is why I almost ignored the interview request from Yan Big Davis.

Yan Big contacted me for the first time through my website on 18 May 2016. He wrote that he wanted to interview me about protest for an organization called Black Matters, an online community that he claimed had 200,000 likes. His email was strange. His English was awkward. I'd never heard of Black Matters but it sounded like a copycat of Black Lives Matter.

My intuition told me to stay away. And initially I did. But two weeks later, on a lark, I wrote back and accepted his request. In a sign of my residual wariness, I scheduled the interview for nearly a month after his original email.

The interview with Yan Big was immediately uncomfortable. The phone quality was terrible: it sounded like he was calling internationally or through a distant internet connection. He had a strange accent and an unusual way of phrasing questions. He was obviously not a typical American.

I rationalized that he must be an African immigrant living in America and that was why he was interested in protesting against racism and police brutality. His attempts at flattery set off more alarm bells. I finished up the interview as quickly as possible and got off the phone.

Yan Big posted the interview on the Black Matters website and for the next few months he emailed me to ask for help promoting protests in America against the continued incarceration of the MOVE 9 and Jerome Skee Smith. I never replied again.

I actively forgot about Yan Big until 18 months later when a reporter with Russia's RBC informed me that Black Matters was a frountgroup run by the nefarious Internet Research Agency, a Russian private intelligence and propaganda firm – a "troll factory" - with deep ties to Vladimir Putin's regime.

Black Matters was one of many fake activist groups, such as Blacktivist and the police brutality tracker DoNotShoot.us, created to mimic and influence American protesters. RBC discovered around 120 Facebook, Twitter and Instagram frontgroup accounts with a combined total of 6 million followers and likes.

As a revolutionary American activist I'd been on guard against domestic intelligence agencies, not foreign governments, and Russia exploited that posture.

The American media started calling me within hours of RBC breaking the story. Russia had attempted to use me for their anti-democratic agenda – rather unsuccessfully as I had stopped replying to their emails – and now the American corporate media was vying to use me for theirs.

BuzzFeed rushed out a report. CNN sent a car to transport me to Time Warner headquarters for an on-camera interview that was instantly uncomfortable in a way oddly reminiscent of my brief encounter with Yan Big.

CNN's interviewer and producer seemed to want me to play the naive victim: angry at the US government for not protecting me and furious at the Silicon Valley tech companies for allowing this to happen. I got the tingly sense and refused this disempowering and anti-revolutionary narrative.

Instead, I gave a nuanced reply and told them I wanted a revolution in America, not a clampdown on social media's role in protest. CNN did not air the interview. The same thing happened when I spoke with a producer of NPR's flagship show All Things Considered.

So what is the American media unwilling to consider?

First of all, Russia's efforts are part of a larger shift in the nature of war in which activists are becoming the pawns of superpowers. We are witnessing the advent of social movement warfare: the deployment of social protest as an effective alternative to conventional military conflict.

Russia's attempts to foment, stage and manage social protest in western democracies is a strategic response to allegedly American-funded "color revolutions" like the Rose, Orange and Tulip revolutions against Russian-allied governments in Georgia (2003-2004), Ukraine (2004-2005) and Kyrgyzstan (2005) along with, arguably, the Arab Spring (2010-2012) and Euromaidan Revolution (2013-2014).

The Russian ministry of defense hosted an international conference in 2014whose primary focus was developing counter-strategies against these color revolutions. And, although this has never been publicly disclosed, it is reasonable to suspect that sparking a color revolution in America was discussed in the backrooms.

I am reluctant to respond to this trend by calling for a ban on foreign support for domestic activism. This kind of meddling might be a necessary evil. I can think of very few successful revolutions that did not rely on foreign aid.

France supported the American Revolution beginning with the Treaty of Amity and Commerce in 1778. Germany, which was at war with Russia, helped Lenin return from exile to lead the Bolshevik Russian Revolution in 1917. The anti-apartheid movement in South Africa received significant international support. Or here is an example close to my heart: Occupy Wall Street, a global movement that ostensibly began in New York City, was actually created by a Canadian magazine.

In fact, although it is rarely discussed, the Occupy movement received substantial support from Russia. I remember how the state-owned RT television station (formerly Russia Today) aggressively supported the movement with hyperbolic coverage of police brutality.

RT even rewarded one prominent Occupy political comedian known for YouTube tirades with his own show, Redacted Tonight. A recent profile of that former activist revealed his now complete reluctance to criticize Putin. And during the height of the movement, RT invited David Graeber and other prominent founding Occupiers from New York City to London to film an episode of Julian Assange's show.

These were all obvious attempts to co-opt our social protest by amplifying it and becoming the movement's primary mouthpiece and media source. But it still helped Occupy spread to 82 countries.

What is qualitatively different about the situation today, and reason for genuine concern among activists, is that Russia now seems less interested in supporting authentic movements and more concerned with outright control.

Russia never tried, as far as we know, to splinter off a fake Occupy frontgroup. Back then Russia wasn't seeking to create American movements directly led and controlled by Russian citizens.

Today, on the contrary, we know that Russians created fake Black Lives Matter protests and fake Standing Rock social media accounts. This shift from providing support to actively establishing groups under their total control is the real danger activists must resist.

From co-opting Occupy to cloning Black Lives Matter, the next step will be the creation of new, previously unheard of, contagious social protests in America that are conceived, designed, launched and remotely controlled entirely by foreign governments.

Many activists might join these protests because they believe in the cause being espoused without realizing who owns the leadership. But if the suspicion becomes widespread that tomorrow's social movements are actually Russian, Chinese or North Korean frontgroups then there will be a profound delegitimization of protest that significantly bolsters the anti-democratic forces in western democracies that already want to clamp down on activism.

Both outcomes represent truly terrifying future scenarios that lead to the most pressing question of all: what can activists do?

The way forward begins with an honest acknowledgement from American activists that we were complicit in Russia's ability to mimic our protest movements. We allowed our techniques of protest to become so entirely predictable that a fake Black Lives Matter group can gain more likes than the real one and an agent in Moscow can organize a plausible protest in Charlotte, North Carolina.

Activism has become scripted and this has increased not only the ineffectiveness of our protests but also our susceptibility to mimicry by external anti-democratic forces. The indistinguishability between fake and real protest is a wake-up call for protesters and must be the catalyst for a profound rethink of contemporary activism.

That is how we protect ourselves. Here is how we fight back.

Genuine social protests tend to boomerang around the world. So let's ensure that foreign governments fear that the protests they create abroad will return home. To protect against fake activism in America we must insist that every protest be globally oriented.

That means exporting our protests to every country, especially those suspected of supporting, co-opting or controlling our movements. If Russia wants to create civil rights protests in Oakland then they must be prepared to deal with those same protests back into Moscow. From this point forward, our best defense is a global offense.

11

Case Studies in Troll Armies Around the World: China

Gary King, Jennifer Pan, and Margaret E. Roberts

Gary King is the Weatherhead University Professor at Harvard University. Jennifer Pan is an assistant professor of communications at Stanford University. Margaret E. Roberts is an assistant professor of political science at University of California, San Diego.

While the international reach of Russia's troll armies has drawn attention to Moscow and St. Petersburg, various other countries have also employed similar techniques to utilize the internet as a vehicle for disseminating state propaganda. One of the most longstanding and notorious government trolling operations has been happening in China since around 2004. Collectively nicknamed the "50c party," Chinese government-sponsored trolling operations are different from their Russian counterparts in their avoidance of the staged political debates for which the IRA has become notorious. Instead, paid commentators—originally thought to be paid "50 cents" per comment—create positive, uplifting content: a collective campaign to diminish political grievances by drowning them out.

The Chinese government has long been suspected of hiring as many as 2,000,000 people to surreptitiously insert huge numbers of pseudonymous and other deceptive writings

Gary King, Jennifer Pan, and Margaret E. Roberts. 2017. "How the Chinese Government Fabricates Social Media Posts for Strategic Distraction, not Engaged Argument." American Political Science Review, 111, 3, pp. 484-501, URL: GaryKing.org/50c.

into the stream of real social media posts, as if they were the genuine opinions of ordinary people. Many academics, and most journalists and activists, claim that these so-called "50c party" posts vociferously argue for the government's side in political and policy debates. As we show, this is also true of the vast majority of posts openly accused on social media of being 50c. Yet, almost no systematic empirical evidence exists for this claim, or, more importantly, for the Chinese regime's strategic objective in pursuing this activity. In the first large scale empirical analysis of this operation, we show how to identify the secretive authors of these posts, the posts written by them, and their content. We estimate that the government fabricates and posts about 448 million social media comments a year. In contrast to prior claims, we show that the Chinese regime's strategy is to avoid arguing with skeptics of the party and the government, and to not even discuss controversial issues. We show that the goal of this massive secretive operation is instead to distract the public and change the subject, as most of the these posts involve cheerleading for China, the revolutionary history of the Communist Party, or other symbols of the regime. We discuss how these results fit with what is known about the Chinese censorship program, and suggest how they may change our broader theoretical understanding of "common knowledge" and information control in authoritarian regimes.

Introduction

Social media in China appears as vibrant and extensive as in any Western country, with more than 1,300 social media companies and websites, and millions of posts authored every day by people all over the country. At the same time, the Chinese regime imposes extensive and varied controls over of the entire system (Brady, 2009; Cairns and Carl- son, 2016; Knockel et al., 2015; MacKinnon, 2012; Jason Q. Ng, 2015; Shirk, 2011; Stockmann, 2013; Stockmann and Gallagher, 2011; G. Yang, 2009). Which social media companies are prevented from operating in China is easy to see (the so-called "Great Firewall of China"), and the scholarly literature now offers considerable evidence on how and why they censor certain individual social media posts that have appeared on the web or filter them out before appearing. In both cases, the censorship apparatus allows a great deal of criticism of the regime, its officials, and their policies (which can be useful information for the central government in managing local leaders) but stops discussions that can generate collective action on the ground (King, Pan, and Roberts, 2013, 2014).[1]

According to numerous speculations by scholars, activists, journalists, officials in other governments, and participants in social media, the Chinese regime also conducts "astroturfing," or what we might call "reverse censorship," surreptitiously posting large numbers of fabricated social media comments, as if they were the genuine opinions of ordinary Chinese people. The people hired for this purpose are known formally as "In- ternet commentators" but more widely as "50c party" members, so-called because they are rumored to be paid 50 cents (5 jiao, or about US$0.08) to write and post each comment (Tong and Lei, 2013). Although we show that this rumor turns out to be incorrect, we adopt this widely used term to denote social media comments posted at the direction or behest of the regime, as if they were the opinions of ordinary people.[2]

[…]

At every stage, our results indicate that prevailing views about the 50c party are largely incorrect. We show that almost none of the Chinese government's 50c party posts engage in debate or argument of any kind. They do not step up to defend the government, its leaders, and their policies from criticism, no matter how vitriolic; indeed, they seem to avoid controversial issues entirely. Instead, most 50c posts are about cheerleading and positive discussions of valence issues. We also detect a high level of coordination in the timing and content in these posts. A theory consistent with these patterns is that the strategic objective of the regime is to distract and redirect public attention from discussions or events with collective action potential.

[…]

Size of the 50c Party

[…]In this section, we study how widespread 50c activity is. Overall, we find a massive government effort, where every year the 50c party writes approximately 448 million social media posts nationwide. About 52.7% of these posts appear on government sites. The remaining 212 million posts are inserted into the stream of approximately 80 billion total posts on commercial social media sites, all in real time. If these estimates are correct, a large proportion of government web site comments, and about one of every 178 social media posts on commercial sites, are fabricated by the government. The posts are not randomly distributed but are highly focused and directed, all with specific intent and content.

[…]

Theoretical Implications

China

One way to parsimoniously summarize existing empirical results about information control in China is with a theory of the strategy of the regime. This theory, which as with all theories is a simplification of the complex realities on the ground, involves two complementary principles the Chinese regime appears to follow, one passive and one active. The passive principle is *do not engage on controversial issues*: do not insert 50c posts supporting, and do not censor posts criticizing, the regime, its leaders, or their policies. The second, active, principle is *stop discussions with collective action potential*, by active distraction and active censorship. Cheerleading in directed 50c bursts is one way the government distracts the public, although this activity can be also be used to distract from general negativity, government related meetings and events with protest potential, etc. (Citizens criticize the regime without collective action on the ground in many ways, including even via unsubstantiated threats of protest and viral bursts of online-only activity — which, by this definition, do not have collective action potential and so are ignored by the government.)

These twin strategies appear to derive from the fact that the main threat perceived by the Chinese regime in the modern era is not military attacks from foreign enemies but rather uprisings from their own people. Staying in power involves managing their government and party agents in China's 32 provincial-level regions, 334 prefecture level divisions, 2,862 county-level divisions, 41,034 township-level administrations, and 704,382 village-level subdivisions, and somehow keeping in check collective action organized by those outside of government. The balance of supportive and critical commentary on social media about specific issues, in specific jurisdictions, is useful to the government in judging the performance of (as well as keeping or replacing) local leaders and ameliorating other information problems faced by central authorities (Dimitrov, 2014a,b,c; Wintrobe, 1998). As such, avoiding any artificial change in that balance — such as from 50c posts or censorship — can be valuable.

Distraction is a clever and useful strategy in information control in that an argument in almost any human discussion is rarely an effective way to put an end to an opposing argument. Letting an argument die, or changing the subject, usually works much better than picking an argument and getting someone's back up (as new parents recognize fast). It may even be the case that the function of reasoning in human beings is fundamentally about winning arguments rather than resolving them by seeking truth (Mercier and Sperber, 2011). Distraction even has the advantage of reducing anger compared to ruminating on the same issue (Denson, Moulds, and Grisham, 2012). Finally, since censorship alone seems to anger people (Roberts, 2015), the 50c astroturfing program has the additional advantage of enabling the government to actively control opinion without having to censor as much as they might otherwise.

Authoritarian Politics

For the literature on authoritarian politics in general, our results may help refine current theories of the role of information, and in particular what is known as "common knowledge," in theories of revolutionary mobilization. Many theories in comparative politics assume that autocrats slow the spread of information critical of the regime in order to minimize the development of common knowledge of grievances which, in turn, may reduce the probability of mobilization against the regime. The idea is that coordination is essential to revolution, and coordination requires some common knowledge of shared grievances (Chwe, 2013; Egorov, Guriev, and Sonin, 2009; Hollyer, Rosendorff, and Vreeland, 2014; Persson and Tabellini, 2006; Tilly, 1978).

In contrast, our results suggest that the Chinese regime differentiates between two types of common knowledge — about specific grievances, which they allow, and about collective action potential, which they do a great deal to avoid. Avoiding the spread of common knowledge about collective action events (and not grievances) is consistent with research by Kuran (1989, 1991), Lohmann (1994), and Lorentzen (2013), who focus specifically on the spread of information about real-world protest and on-going collective action rather than the generic spread of common knowledge more broadly.

The idea is that numerous grievances of a population ruled autocratically by non- elected leaders are obvious and omnipresent. Learning of one more grievance, in and of itself, should have little impact on the power of a potential revolutionary to ignite protest. The issue, then, appears not to be whether such grievances are learned by large enough numbers to foment a revolution. Instead, we can think of creative political actors, including those aspiring to lead a revolution or coup, as treating issues, ideologies, events, arguments, ideas, and grievances as "hooks on which politicians hang their objectives and by which they further their interests," including interests that entail initiating or fostering a political uprising (Shepsle, 1985). If one hook is not available, they can use another.

By this logic, then, common knowledge of grievances is already commonplace and so allowing more information about them to become public is of little risk to the regime or value to its opponents. Since disrupting discussion of grievances only limits information that is otherwise useful to the regime, the leaders have little reason to censor it, argue with it, or flood the net with opposing viewpoints. What *is* risky for the regime, and therefore vigorously opposed through large scale censorship and huge numbers of fabricated social media posts, is posts with collective action potential.

[…]

Notes

[1] While we make general statements about Chinese censorship, it is important to note that censorship in China is by no means monolithic in its operations or outcomes. Censorship is largely carried out by internet content providers, and regulations over the flow of information continues to evolve. As a result, there is variation in the precise details of censorship in China by platform, geography, and over time.

[2] Thus, 50c party members are distinct from "volunteer 50c members" (known as "bring your own grainers"), who express pro-regime or anti-western sentiment online without being paid by the government, the "little red flowers", an unpaid red guard who also attack opponents of the regime online, the "American Cent Party" who express western democratic values and criticize the Chinese communist regime online, and the "internet water army", which refers to for-hire astroturfers working for and advancing the interests of companies and other actors willing to pay their fees. None are known to be organized groups. Of course, political parties do not exist in China and so, despite the name, the "50c Party" is not a political party. For an excellent overview of the purpose and tactics of the volunteer 50c party, see Han (2015a)

12

Case Studies in Troll Armies Around the World: The Philippines

Chay F. Hofileña

Chay F. Hofileña is Investigative Desk Head at Rappler, an award-winning Filipino news website founded by Maria Ressa.

In 2016, the Filipino news website Rappler *began identifying thousands of fake Facebook accounts that had been generated prior to that year's presidential election. Sporting profile pictures of attractive celebrities and friend lists full of other "sock puppet" accounts, many of these were traced to volunteers for Rodrigo Duterte's campaign, a tactic that campaign aides admitted was pursued in lieu of more expensive and traditional political advertising strategies such as buying TV spots. But even after Duterte's victory, many of these troll accounts continue to be run by former members of his campaign in order "to allow Duterte to effectively govern."*

Create false perceptions. This is what a network of combined real and fake accounts on social media can achieve in a matter of minutes.

Over the past several weeks, we monitored several suspicious accounts connected to various online Facebook groups.

One account alone we determined to be fake was connected (as of October 6, 2016) to about 2.9 million members of various overseas Filipino groups associated with Ferdinand "Bongbong"

"Fake accounts, manufactured reality on social media," by Chay F. Hofileña, Rappler, October 9, 2016. Reprinted by permission.

Marcos Jr, and other hobby groups. Another fake account was linked to over 990,000 members of groups supporting President Rodrigo Duterte, and still another was connected to an estimated 3.8 million members of various overseas Filipino organizations and buy-and-sell groups.

Imagine the impact of a single message sent from just one fake account and spread to these hundreds of thousands of Facebook accounts. Even assuming only 10% actually share a post by a fake account, the spread of wrong information can still be damaging. They can convincingly manufacture reality on social media as they wish, transforming perception to reality, and swaying opinion on the basis of perceived number and power.

In the Philippines, with a population of 100 million, there are an estimated 47 million active Facebook accounts as of 2015.

In the 2016 elections, Facebook recorded about 22 million Filipino Facebook users interacting and actively talking about, and debating over the elections with friends and their respective connections. Yet, most political campaigners belittled the ability of social media to sway voters and influence voting – some political camps said it was just all noise with little power for conversion.

Something interesting happened, however, in the last quarter of 2015, as candidates geared up for the campaign.

Nest of "Sock Puppets"

John Victorino, an investment analyst who has been working overseas for the last 7 years, and who has monitored a nest of online accounts for at least 3 months already, spotted some noticeable patterns in what he described as suspicious accounts.

He called them "sock puppets" or fake accounts. Sock puppets are used to either amplify a message, drown out a contrary or conflicting message, or even create a false sense of the popularity of an idea or cause through amplification and spread.

Some of these sock puppets, aptly named because they act according to how a puppeteer motions them, post in existing online forums on Facebook – political groups, hobbyists, buy-and-sell, and even OFW groups, Victorino observed. The infiltration is subtle, and the undiscerning could very well fall into the trap of interacting with and helping create activity within a group or discussion thread.

Victorino said some of the accounts he watched closely were created fairly recently, in the last quarter of 2015, in the lead up to the May 2016 elections. Those who were part of this nest shared common practices:

- They used profile photos of celebrities or other sexy-looking persons instead of their own
- They used cover photos like gardens and foreign sceneries that were shared among them and their supposed friends
- They had similar liked pages such as Okay Dito and Ask Philippines
- They had less than 50 friends

One of them, linked to groups whose members number over 2.8 million as of early October, is a certain "Mutya Bautista", a supposed software analyst at ABS-CBN. She uses the profile picture of pop star Im Yoona of Girl's Generation, a South Korean KPop group, and has ties to over 160 groups – the biggest of which is BongBong Marcos United at over 160,000 members, and other overseas Filipino workers groups like Pinoy OFW sa UAE with over 67,000 members.

A check with ABS-CBN showed that "Mutya Bautista," who has only 21 friends, was and is not connected with the media giant, just like several others such as "Jovelyn Mayor", "Lenny de Jesus", "Babylyn Ventura", "Kim Montes", and "Julius Marquez" who all also claimed to be with ABS-CBN.

"Lily Lopez" also declared herself to be connected with Xurpas Inc. But she's not. She used as her profile picture the photo of former Miss Korea and now actress Kim Sa-rang. She also happens to be a Facebook "friend" of the fake "Mutya Bautista".

Another interesting profile is that of "Luvimin Cancio", who sourced her profile photo from softcorecams.com. This was established via tineye.com. She has 46 friends – many of them sock puppets too sharing the same characteristics, and some of them appearing to be real people.

A fourth Facebook account, that of "Jasmin De La Torre", shows the exact same cover photo as Lily Lopez. She only has 14 friends as of October 7 but is a member of various groups whose members total almost a million.

There is also the account of "Raden Alfaro Payas", who has links to over 200 groups with over 3.8 million members. Raden uses another profile picture also of Im Yoona. He however describes himself as a senior engineer at Northrup Grumman Corporation and lives in Grand Rapids, Michigan. This account has 49 friends as of October 5, about 13 of them part of the nest of 26 sock puppets watched closely by Victorino. Among Raden's friends is someone with an identical name but who appears to be a real person.

The same real person Raden has over 1,300 friends, among them at least 16 with fake accounts. He also creates a page as a public figure with likes of over 1,200 people.

How Falsehood Spreads

To illustrate how one misleading and false information can be spread using a mix of trolls and real people, Victorino pointed to identical posts by "Mutya Bautista" and the real person Raden Alfaro Payas shared with the groups BongBong Marcos United and Bongbong Marcos Loyalist Facebook Warriors last June.
Similarly there was a post from the fake account of "Luvimin Cancio" on the Rody R. Duterte Movement group about "alleged martial law victims" posted last September 28 on a blog, why0why. com.

The blog also said: "Martial law victims should tell young generation that 'pasaway kami kaya kami nakulong.'" (We were belligerent that's why we were imprisoned.)

Affirmed by what appears to be another account of Raden Alfaro Payas, created only last September 21, information about victims of Martial Law is twisted and reaffirmed by another troll or fake account.

Efficient Use of Social Media

Social media by itself can be empowering for the disadvantaged and those without access to mainstream media.

For instance, Nic Gabunada, who was part of the presidential campaign of then Davao mayor Rodrigo Duterte, said limited campaign funds forced them to be creative in using the social media space. Duterte's campaign budget was nowhere near the budget of other presidential contenders, if political ads were any indication. In the past, presidential campaigns were said to cost anywhere between P1 billion to P3 billion.

In an interview last June with Rappler, Gabunada, who was part of the Duterte campaign communications team, said his P10-million budget allowed him to tap into a robust volunteer network of about 400-500 whose individual networks at the time of the campaign reached hundreds of thousands – the largest group having about 800,000 members.

It was these "warriors" on social media who delivered the presidency to Duterte, who won with over 16.6 million votes – convincingly and overwhelmingly over his strongest rival Manuel "Mar" Roxas II who got over 9.9 million votes.

In contrast, the battle for the vice presidency was intense and breathlessly close between Leni Robredo of the Liberal Party and Marcos. Robredo edged out Marcos, garnering 14.4 million votes compared to his 14.2 million votes.

Duterte campaign insiders admitted they used trolls or fake accounts and paid for them, along with "influencers" on social media, essentially people or accounts that had a huge following. There was no unanimity of opinion within the Duterte camp, however, as some like Duterte social media director Pompee La Viña were reported to have favored more engagement over the use of trolls.

It was Gabunada who had part command over the efficient network that included overseas Filipino workers (OFWs) and even regional groups in Luzon, Visayas, and Mindanao. During the campaign, there were messages of the week or of the month cascaded to what he called "parallel groups" or the Duterte "warriors".

They had administrator or "admin coordinators" in various chat rooms that already existed. A chat group of admins constituted the "super admins".

Gabunada explained that it could be a chat group of 20 people who could each be administering two to 5 chat groups or pages "Their whole principle is organizing for social media effectiveness," Gabunada said.

But even after an overwhelming victory with over 16 million votes, Gabunada explained there was a need to continue campaigning because they got "only 40% of the votes" and needed more than that to allow Duterte to effectively govern.

He admitted there were some groups "*[na] talagang palaban, matigas ulo* (really combative, hard-headed)…sometimes we felt they were out of control so *mahirap ma-associate doon* (it was hard to be associated with them)."

At the time, they were also suspicious of other camps doing counter propaganda. And they could be at play even today, Duterte supporters say.

Fast-forward to the present, months after Duterte won as president, there is evidence that trolls are still very much alive. These trolls "seed" messages taken from blogs and pages, and which are then amplified by other trolls and spread through members of bigger groups. The messages are beneficial to various political camps and interests, creating a false notion of what is true and what is real.

Propaganda Agents and Propagators

In addition to the activities of the trolls, there are also noticeable "propaganda pages" associated with Duterte.

In September of this year, du30newsinfo.com was observed to have at least 13 agents or spammers who posted over 4,000 posts in more than 40 groups. An account is classified as an agent or spammer if it had posted more than 100 items in groups in a single month from a single website or page alone. The 4,000 posts resulted in a cumulative 170,000-plus shares. This means that one post alone generated an average of over 40 shares. At least five of these posts received more than 1,000 shares. This is how one post can go viral very quickly.

Besides that, newsph.info, with only 5 agents generated over 50,000 shares from only 1,300 posts during the same period. Similarly, nowreader.com generated 39,000 shares from over 1,100 posts of only 3 agents.

In the same month, the site whose content is regularly shared by the troll Luvimin Cancio, OKD2.com, got 11,900 shares from only 716 posts.

From August 1 to September 20, some accounts were observed to be sharing the same links more than 7 times on average with different groups. Our tally showed that each of the top 10 "spammers" who mentioned Senator Leila de Lima, a recent favorite, posted at least 200 messages during that period.

Interestingly, on October 5, one account was observed to be sharing a link about alleged drug lord Jaybee Sebastian to 23 different groups in rapid succession, merely copy-pasting text for each post. The interval of posts varied from 3 seconds to 6 minutes based on time stamps.

The frequency of posts of sock puppets and real persons alike indicate any of several things:

- posters who pretty much post and share content to their liking throughout the day are dedicated followers or supporters of whoever they are supporting
- posts are automated
- posts can be misused as an effective tool of harassment
- posters copy-paste and share content for a living

'Business Partners'

How much are trolls paid – whether for political or commercial purposes?

In one page for commercial purposes, for example, repeated call-outs were made for "business partners" who were required in 2015 to spend 3-5 hours daily on Facebook. Payment was supposed to range conservatively from P1,000 a day to P10,000 a month, with training provided.

The *Inquirer* had reported that some trolls even get paid from P2,000 to P3,000 a day just by copy-pasting content. This explains the uniform posts or comments seen on Facebook. Clearly, trolling has become and can become an even more lucrative business.

The danger of propagators spreading false or misleading information is all too evident. It can result in beliefs or convictions anchored on false premises. Different versions of what is supposed to be the one true fact can be manufactured, creating confusion and deep-seated schisms among groups who get to believe that their version of the truth is what is real and correct.

[…]

13

The Redistribution of Information

Branko Milanovic

Branko Milanovic is a Serbian-American economist. His most notable book is The Haves and the Have-Nots: A Brief and Idiosyncratic History of Global Inequality.

Web brigades—in Russia and elsewhere—are perceived as a threat to democracy because of their behind-the-scenes manipulation of information through using troll accounts to spread fake news stories on trusted websites. Branko Milanovic provides a way to look at the crisis of fake news within the context of the larger history of global media. Before the internet, Milanovic notes, communicating seemingly credible news required massive amounts of capital. The internet reduced these costs and eroded what he calls the global Western monopoly on information. For the first time in recent history, American audiences are being subjected to the influence of non-Western media creating "narratives of America," which consequently influences our own conversations.

Very few people can make sense of the current "fake news" hysteria and almost nobody is willing to look at it in a historical context and to understand why the problem arose now.

The reason why the hysteria has spread, and especially so in the United States, is because this is (to some extend understandable)

"'Fake News': Reaction to the end of the monopoly on the narrative," by Branko Milanovic, LUISS Guido Carli, March 29, 2018, http://open.luiss.it/en/2018/03/29/listeria-sulle-fake-news-nasce-perche-i-media-classici-hanno-perso-il-loro-monopolio-sullinformazione/. Licensed under CC BY 3.0 IT.

reaction to the loss of global monopoly power exercised by the Anglo-American media especially since 1989, but practically from 1945 onwards.

The reasons for the Western quasi-monopoly between 1949 and 1989 (call it Phase1) were manifold: much greater amount of information provided by outlets like BBC, and later CNN, than national outlets in many countries; much broader reach of large English-language media services· they were covering all countries when national media could barely pay correspondents to be located in two or three top world capitals; spread of English as the second language; and last but not least, better quality of the news (say, greater truthfulness) than found in national sources.

These advantages of Western media were especially obvious for the citizens of the Second World where governments maintained tight censorship and thus the USSR had even to go to the extremes of jamming Western radio-stations. But even in the rest of the world the Western media was often better than local media for the reasons I mentioned.

A careful reader will have noticed that so far I contrasted global Anglo-American media to national or local media only. This is because only the former had a global reach and the rest of the media (due to lack of finances or ambition, government control or small languages) were purely national. So the US and English media fought a rather one-sided battle with small national newspapers or TVs. It is no surprise that the global Anglo-American media was then able to control, in many cases fully, political narratives. Not only were Western media totally able to influence what (say) people in Zambia thought of Argentina or the reverse (because there was probably next to zero local coverage available to somebody living in Zambia regarding what is happening in Argentina; and the reverse); more importantly, because of Western media's greater openness and better quality, they were able to influence even the narrative within Zambia or within Argentina.

The global competitors that the West faced in that period were laughable. Chinese, Soviet and Albanian short-wave radios had programs in multiple languages but their stories were so stultifying, boring and unrealistic that people who, from time to time, listened to them did it mostly for amusement purposes.

The Western media monopoly then expanded even further with the fall of Communism (call it Phase 2). All the formerly Communist countries where citizens used clandestinely to listen to Radio Free Europe were now more than willing to believe in the truth of everything being uttered by London and Washington. Many of these outlets installed themselves in the former Eastern Bloc (RFE is headquartered now in Prague).

But that honeymoon of global Western monopoly began to change when the "others" realized that they too could try to become global in a single media space that was created thanks to globalization and internet. Spread of the internet insured that you could produce Spanish- or Arabic-language shows and news and be watched anywhere in the world. Al Jazeera was the first to significantly dent, and then destroy, the western monopoly on the Middle Eastern narrative in the Middle East. And now we enter Phase 3. Turkish, Russian and Chinese channels then did the same. What happened in the news was paralleled in another area where Anglo-American monopoly was also total but then got eroded. Global TV series that were exported used to be only US- or UK-produced; but soon they got very successful competitors in Latin American telenovelas, Indian and Turkish series, and more recently Russian. Actually, these newcomers practically pushed US and UK series almost altogether from their "domestic" markets (which, for example, for Turkey includes most of the Middle East and the Balkans).

Then came the Phase 4 when other non-Western media realized that they could try to challenge Western news monopoly not only outside but on the Western media home-turf. This is when Al Jazeera-US, Russia Today, CCTV and others entered with their English-language (and then French, Spanish etc.) shows and news directed toward global, including American, audience.

This was indeed an enormous change. And this is why we are now going through a phase of hysterical reaction to the "fake news": because it is the first time that non-Western media are not only creating their own global narratives but are also trying to create narratives of America.

For people from small countries (like myself) this is just something totally normal: we are used to foreigners not only appointing our ministers but being present throughout the media space, and even influencing, often because the quality of their news and scholarship is better, the narrative about country's own history or politics. But for many people in the US and the UK this comes as a total shock: how dare foreigners tell them what is the narrative of their own countries?

There are two possible outcomes. One is that the US public will have to realize that, with globalization on, even the most important country like the US is not immune from the influences of others; even the US becomes, compared to the world as a whole, "small". Another possibility is that the hysteria will lead to the fragmentation of the Internet space as China, Saudi Arabia and others are already doing. Then instead of a nice global platform for all opinions, we shall be back to the pre-1945 situation with national "radio stations", local internets, bans of foreign languages (and perhaps even foreigners) on national NatNets—basically we shall have ended globalization of free thinking and gone back to unadulterated nationalism.

14

Understanding Media in the Era of "Fake News"

Madeleine Crean

Madeleine Crean is a former intern at the Post-Conflict Research Centre in Sarajevo and holds an MA in Media and the Middle East from the School of Oriental and African Studies in London.

With greater attention being paid to "fake news" and government propaganda that is peddled as news, media consumers have become increasingly concerned about finding ways to reduce the impact of fake news and propaganda and cut through the noise. Crean argues that the best way to do this is through being a critical media consumer who knows how to understand a news story and the ways journalists (or trolls) are trying to influence their audience. Through understanding the means of distorting events and stories, media consumers can better understand the facts and ignore the opinions being forced upon them, which would help them to learn more from real news and ignore fake news.

In an era when "fake news" is at the forefront of discussion and constant Internet access is providing us with an unprecedented flow of information, news media confronts us with many different depictions of reality. Control over mass media narratives gives media producers the capacity to influence what the public believes about what is happening in their localities and across the world.

Media has the power to shape how the public understands a story. In addition, how a story is told is greatly influenced by the person telling the story, their individual experiences, what internalized beliefs they hold and who they are writing for. Each person observes a situation through his or her own unique lens. There are many subtle biases that make their way into how a story is presented by the media. Outlined below are some important things media consumers should keep in mind while reading the news.

What Is Included and What Is Not?

News can easily be distorted by excluding or obscuring certain elements of the story. For example, a right-leaning newspaper may omit some policy objectives of a left-wing politician in order to highlight the negatives. This was directly evident in media coverage of Labour Party leader Jeremy Corbyn's (United Kingdom) political views. A London School of Economics study[1] found that "three-quarters of newspaper stories about Jeremy Corbyn in the first months of his leadership either distorted or failed to represent his actual views on subjects." Corbyn's views were presented without alteration in just 11 per cent of news stories. They were otherwise taken out of context or distorted. As a critical reader, it is important to check multiple sources when reading a story and to keep in mind what some papers are including and excluding. By reading multiple sources, you can weave together your own understanding of the story and why different media actors are presenting the narrative the way they are. Competing parties have a vested interest in monopolizing public opinion and making sure that people are sympathetic to their version of events and that their actions are seen as legitimate and right. Today, power relations are increasingly played out in the realm of communication as a struggle to monopolize public opinion.

How Are Actors Framed?

Different people can be depicted as relatable or not, good or bad, with a few simple tactics. What language is used to describe them? Which actions are they focusing on? How are they being framed? Are they using photos that make the subject look aggressive or friendly and relatable? Frames are used to narrate events in a way that can encourage a specific reaction or interpretation from its given audience. Without necessarily completely obscuring historical events, news producers may select elements that will contribute to a certain reaction and that will fit their version of right and wrong. Narratives may highlight the wrongdoing of some over others, obscuring the wrongdoer's own failures and exaggerating the importance of certain events to create a story that makes sense to the audience. For example, before the Syrian Civil War began in 2011, the Obama administration was interested in improving ties with the Syrian regime. Bashar and Asma al-Assad are quite westernized, educated and at ease in cosmopolitan European cities. These traits were emphasized during periods of positive Syrian-American relations. Asma al-Assad was seen as an elegant and stylish first lady. As soon as civil war broke out in 2011 and the US sided with the rebels, American media tended to depict Bashar and Asma as a greedy, bloodthirsty couple. Asma, once praised by fashion magazines, was then condemned for lavish spending on clothes and furniture with stolen Syrian money.[2]

What Kind of Language Is Used to Sway Opinion?

The language used to describe people and events subtly (or not so subtly) skews how we interpret the news. Certain words can be used to tip off the reader as to whether they should interpret the story as good or bad, legitimate or illegitimate. For example, if the actors involved in a bombing are labeled "freedom fighters", we are bound to think of the event much differently than if they are labeled "terrorists". Consider the use of language by UK newspaper *The Independent* in their coverage of Labour Party leader Jeremy Corbyn's manifesto: "For the many, not the few". *The Independent* claims: "Whatever you thought of Jeremy Corbyn before, you can't deny the manifesto delivers." "For the many, not the few" has turned out to be more than just a slogan, unlike Theresa May's repetitive use of the phrase: "strong and stable". Using language such as, "can't deny" strongly props Corbyn up. In contrast, May is accused of "constant parroting", which serves to delegitimize her message by implying she is repetitious and even annoying.[3]

How Are Events Framed?

The media use culturally resonant frames to appeal to their target audience. When a historical event is transformed into a mediated narrative, it must carry a decodable message to have an effect on the audience, that is, something culturally and socially relatable to the audience. The narrative must be associated with a certain discourse that can be, in turn, realized and decoded by the consumer. Producers incorporate their knowledge of the social relations of the wider target society into the narratives they produce, which further reproduces a dominant ideology. Media, thus, creates a story that is in line with the power relations of the time as well as something that is digestible and unchallenging for its audience. Cultural norms, recognizable images, and language will add salience to a story. Robert Entman claims that a person's cultural knowledge is part of their "schema", which stores substantive beliefs, preferences, values, attitudes and rules for linking new ideas. These schemas guide the interpretation of messages. Linking frames with culturally embedded schema make them more effective.[4] For example, let's imagine the coverage of a protest in the Middle East carried out by Western media. It would be more effective to highlight the democratic demands of protesters. In contrast, if the same protest were to be covered by a newspaper in the Gulf, it may be more effective to highlight religious elements.

Let's revisit the example of the Assad family. *Vogue* published an article about the Assad family shortly before the conflict erupted, but in March 2011, when the civil uprising began, the article was quickly pulled from the shelves. In the article, Asma is portrayed as both a stylish, professional and dedicated family woman. The writer describes the Assad household as one that is familiar and relatable to an American reader: "there's a decorated Christmas tree, seven-year-old Zein watches Tim Burton's *Alice in Wonderland* on the president's iMac... the household is run on wildly democratic principles."[5] As previously outlined, frames are most effective when they are culturally salient to the consumers. The reference to a Christmas tree, a Hollywood film, democracy, and an iMac computer contrasts the Assad family with an Orientalized idea of an Arab Muslim family that is hostile to and distant from Christian traditions and American culture. This evokes a feeling of closeness and familiarity to the American reader. Orientalism often portrays non-Western women as "ignorant, poor, uneducated, tradition-bound, deistic, family-oriented, victimized, etc." and Western women as "educated, modern, having control over their own bodies and sexualities, and possessing the freedom to make their own decisions."[6] Asma al-Assad is predominantly portrayed as the latter. This portrayal of Asma is effectively used so that she is more closely identified as one of "us" Westerners as opposed to one of "those" backward, hostile Arabs. Orientalism is applied through the lens of Western cultural hegemony, therefore, to make Asma appealing as a soft power capable of contributing to change in Syria, it is most effective to highlight her Western values.

Which Photos Are Being Used to Represent People?

We can say something completely different about someone depending on what photo is used to represent them. The facial expressions that are captured can be used to soften or harden their image. Lighting, depth and exposure of the photo can drastically change the impression the image makes as well. The photo selected to represent the story gives us a visual element to what we are about to read and it can be very powerful. If the media narrative has something negative to say about an event, it is probable that the image will reflect that.

While everything we read may not be entirely objective, that does not mean it is wrong. What it does mean is that we need to remain critical readers. Being informed is more complex than simply reading the news. Whether you are reading something that aligns with your worldview or not, be aware that the way in which a story is told is influenced by the opinions, experiences and beliefs of its producer.

Notes

[1] http://www.independent.co.uk/news/uk/politics/jeremy-corbyn-media-bias-attacks-75-per-cent-three-quarters-fail-to-accurately-report-a7140681.html?cmpid=facebook-post

[2] http://www.huffingtonpost.com/2012/03/20/asma-assad-eu-sanctions-blacklist_n_1366918.html

[3] http://www.independent.co.uk/voices/jeremy-corbyn-labour-manifesto-announcement-whats-in-it-policies-it-delivers-a7738366.html, Liam Young, 16 May 2017

[4] Entman, R. (1989). How the Media Affect What People Think: An Information Processing Approach. *The Journal of Politics*, 51(02), p.347.

[5] http://gawker.com/asma-al-assad-a-rose-in-the-desert-1265002284

[6] Mohanty, C. (1984). Under Western Eyes: Feminist Scholarship and Colonial Discourses. *boundary 2*, 12(3), p, 333

Organizations to Contact

The editors have compiled the following list of organizations concerned with the issues debated in this book. The descriptions are derived from materials provided by the organizations. All have publications or information available for interested readers. The list was compiled on the date of publication of the present volume; the information provided here may change. Be aware that many organizations take several weeks or longer to respond to inquiries, so allow as much time as possible.

Alliance for Securing Democracy
German Marshall Fund 1744 R St., NW
Washington, DC 20009
phone: (202) 683-2650
email: info@gmfus.org
website: securingdemocracy.gmfus.org

Founded shortly after the 2016 election to counter Russian influence on the US and Europe, the Alliance for Securing Democracy was organized and developed by former US State Department officials. It is most well known for the Hamilton 68 dashboard on its website. Here, the Alliance for Securing Democracy publically tracks the activity of hundreds of Twitter accounts that it believes are run in some way by the Russian government. On the website's public dashboard you can track in real time the issues, hashtags, and websites these purportedly Russian accounts are tweeting about and linking to.

Atlantic Council

1030 15th St. NW 12th floor
Washington, DC 20005
phone: (202) 778-4952
email: info@AtlanticCouncil.org
website: www.atlanticcouncil.org

The Atlantic Council is a DC-based think tank that was founded in the early postwar era to advance relations between the United States and Europe. More recently, the Atlantic Council founded the Digital Forensic Research Lab (which can be found at medium.com/dfrlab), a group of researchers who monitor international conflicts in the digital realm. One of their projects, #ElectionWatch, works to "identify, expose, and explain disinformation during elections around the world," and is currently working with Facebook to monitor and expose disinformation surrounding elections on the platform.

The Computational Propaganda Research Project

1 St. Giles
Oxford OX1 3JS
United Kingdom
phone: +44 (0)1865 287210
email: press@oii.ox.ac.uk
website: http://comprop.oii.ox.ac.uk

Part of the University of Oxford's Internet Institute, the Computational Propaganda Research Project was founded in 2012 to investigate the use of "algorithms, automation and computational propaganda in public life." Ultimately aimed at providing information to help common citizens distinguish bot-fuelled online content from actual civil discourse, members of the project are often cited by journalists reporting on breaking political news in order to similarly parse the discourse. Much of its research is made publically available online, along with short videos on subjects like "Is Social Media Killing Democracy?" and "The Digital Origins Of Democracy."

The East StratCom Task Force

Rond Point Robert Schuman 9A
1046 Brussels
Belgium
phone: +32 2584-1111
email: disinforeview@euvsdisinfo.eu
website: https://euvsdisinfo.eu

The East StratCom Task Force is a European Union organization expressly founded in 2015 to, in its own words, "address Russia's ongoing disinformation campaigns." It does this through an online publication called the *Disinformation Review*. Targeting Armenia, Azerbaijan, Belarus, Georgia, Moldova, and Ukraine, the *Review* focuses on correcting "disinformation narratives." The Task Force also maintains a vigorous presence on Twitter and Facebook, with actively maintained verified accounts on both platforms under the handle @EUvsDisinfo.

EastWest Institute

708 Third Ave, Suite 1105
New York, NY 10017
phone: (212) 824-4100
email: newyork@eastwest.ngo
website: www.eastwest.ngo

A nonpartisan think tank formed during the Reagan years, the EastWest Institute focuses on providing diplomatic space for negotiations between major American and Russian parties. In 2016, the EastWest Institute co-founded the Global Commission on the Stability of Cyberspace, a research arm that has published reports on subjects like "Protecting the Electoral Process and its Institutions" and has issued a "Call to Protect the Public Core of the Internet."

Freedom House
1850 M Street NW, Suite 1100
Washington, DC
phone: (202) 296-5101
email: info@freedomhouse.org
website: freedomhouse.org

Every year, this DC-based think tank issues *Freedom on the Net*, its report on how governments around the world manipulate internet discourse to satisfy political ends. Beginning in 2013, these reports began to take notice of "paid pro-government commentators" at work in 22 different countries around the world, including Russia and China. As such, Freedom House takes the view that this kind of government intrusion represents a less free internet and continues to monitor these kind of activities.

Global Engagement Center
email: GEC-IAF@state.gov
website: www.state.gov/r/gec/

Unlike in Russia, US law officially prohibits the government from sponsoring propaganda campaigns targeting its own citizens, but this doesn't mean that the US government doesn't utilize web brigades of its own. In the past, United States Military Central Command has utilized trolling campaigns to counter online propaganda from organizations like ISIS and, more recently, the Global Engagement Center was set up by the State Department to counter disinformation campaigns from Moscow. It has been criticized, however, for its lack of action during the Trump administration so far.

Institute of Modern Russia
231 W 29th St.
New York, NY 10001
phone: (212) 381-2118
email: office@imrussia.org
website: https://imrussia.org/en/

Starting in 2013, this New York-based think tank began a project of translating news articles from major Russian websites and newspapers. Called the *Interpreter*, it would eventually publish a report called "The Menace of Unreality: How the Kremlin Weaponizes Information, Culture and Money," a study of the Kremlin's propaganda abilities in the twenty-first century. Later, the Institute of Modern Russia would itself investigate the use of web brigades in manipulating the discourse surrounding Russia's invasion of the Ukraine.

Moy Rayon

11-Ya Liniya Vasil'yevskogo Ostrova, 66
Saint Petersburg, Russia 199178
phone: (812) 325-25-15
email: web@mr7.ru
website: mr7.ru

One of the few independent news organizations still operating in Russia, it maintains a critical eye on the Kremlin. Its biggest story arrived when it published documents provided by Lyudmila Savchuk, who had worked undercover at an IRA troll farm. It was one of the first stories to provide an inside look at the sophistication of Russian troll operations, and the story surfaced again in 2018, when it was cited in Robert Mueller's FBI investigation of the 2016 presidential election. In a Russian media climate where journalists that aren't controlled by Putin are few and far between, *Moy Rayon* is one of the few remaining watchdogs of civil democracy.

Poynter International Fact Checking Network

The Poynter Institute
801 Third Street
South St. Petersburg, FL 33701
phone: (727) 821-9494
email: info@poynter.org
website: www.poynter.org/channels/fact-checking

Almost as soon as the internet became the most popular way to share information, people began to realize that a lot of that information was false. And almost as quickly the fact-checking website was born, providing deliberately un-sensationalized databases of information. These ranged from Snopes.com to Wikipedia to PolitiFact, which was awarded a Pulitzer Prize in 2009 for its fact-checking during the 2008 US Presidential campaign. Founded in 2015, Poynter's International Fact Checking Network is an effort to bring these diverse intuitions together and give them a more global focus. Poynter, a journalism school in Florida, also owns the *Tampa Bay Times* and runs PolitiFact.

Radio Free Europe/Radio Liberty
1201 Connecticut Ave NW, Ste. 400
Washington, DC 20036
phone: (202) 457-6900
email: webteam@rferl.org
website: pressroom.rferl.org

Radio Free Europe was originally a front for the CIA designed to broadcast anti-Communist propaganda into Eastern Europe. After the end of the Cold War, its main headquarters moved to Prague and its mission evolved toward targeting countries like Azerbaijan and Saddam-era Iraq. More recently, its focus has moved back to Russia, taking over the Institute of Modern Russia's the *Interpreter* and launching polygraph.info, a fact-checking website aimed directly at verifying or correcting claims passed around in Russian media circles.

Bibliography

Books

Ladislav Bittman. *The KGB and Soviet Disinformation*, New York. NY: Pergamon/Brassey's, 1983.

Todd C. Helmus, Elizabeth Bodine-Baron, Andrew Radin, Madeline Magnuson, Joshua Mendelsohn, William Marcellino, Andriy Bega, and Zev Winkelman. *Russian Social Media Influence: Understanding Russian Propaganda in Eastern Europe*. Santa Monica, CA: RAND Corporation, 2018.

Michael Isikoff and David Corn. *Russian Roulette: The Inside Story of Putin's War on America and the Election of Donald Trump*. New York, NY: Twelve, 2018.

Steven Lee Myers. *The New Tsar: The Rise and Reign of Vladimir Putin*. New York, NY: Penguin Random House, 2015.

Malcolm Nance. *The Plot to Destroy Democracy: How Putin and His Spies Are Undermining America and Dismantling the West*. New York, NY: Hachette, 2018.

Arkady Ostrovsky. *The Invention of Russia: From Gorbachev's Freedom to Putin's War*. New York, NY: Penguin Random House, 2016.

Christopher Sampson, ed. *Putin's Asymmetric Assault on Democracy in Russia and Europe: Implications for U.S. National Security*. New York, NY: Skyhorse, 2018.

Andrei Soldatov and Irina Borogan. *The Red Web: The Struggle Between Russia's Digital Dictators and the New Online Revolutionaries*. New York, NY: PublicAffairs, 2015.

Wenfang Tang and Shanto Iyengar, eds. *Political Communication in China: Convergence or Divergence*

Between the Media and Political System? New York, NY: Routledge, 2012.

Periodicals and Internet Sources

Seth Borenstein, "Study finds false stories travel way faster than the truth," *Associated Press*, March 8, 2018, https://www.apnews.com/8da97e49a9064b36baa047d98bb72272/Study-finds-false-stories-travel-way-faster-than-the-truth.

Samantha Bradshaw and Philip N. Howard, "Troops, Trolls and Troublemakers: A Global Inventory of Organized Social Media Manipulation," University of Oxford, Computational Propaganda Research Project, July 2017, http://comprop.oii.ox.ac.uk/wp-content/uploads/sites/89/2017/07/Troops-Trolls-and-Troublemakers.pdf.

Fruzsina Eordogh, "The Russian Troll Army Isn't The Only One We Need To Worry About," *Forbes*, April 11, 2018, https://www.forbes.com/sites/fruzsinaeordogh/2018/04/11/the-russian-troll-army-isnt-the-only-one-we-need-to-worry-about/.

Lauren Etter, "What Happens When the Government Uses Facebook as a Weapon?" *Bloomberg*, December 7, 2017, https://www.bloomberg.com/news/features/2017-12-07/how-rodrigo-duterte-turned-facebook-into-a-weapon-with-a-little-help-from-facebook.

Conor Friedersdorf, "Trump and Russia Both Seek to Exacerbate the Same Political Divisions," the *Atlantic*, January 23, 2018, https://www.theatlantic.com/politics/archive/2018/01/trump-russia-twitter/551093/.

April Glaser, "Reddit Is Finally Reckoning With How It Helped Spread Russian Propaganda in 2016," *Slate*, March 5, 2018, https://slate.com/technology/2018/03/reddit-is-reckoning-with-how-it-helped-spread-russian-propaganda-in-2016.html.

Raju Gopalakrishnan, "Indian journalists say they intimidated, ostracized if they criticize Modi and the BJP," *Reuters*, https://www.reuters.com/article/us-india-politics-media-analysis/indian-journalists-say-they-intimidated-ostracized-if-they-criticize-modi-and-the-bjp-idUSKBN1HX1F4.

Andrew Higgins, "Effort to Expose Russia's 'Troll Army' Draws Vicious Retaliation," *New York Times*, May 30, 2016, https://www.nytimes.com/2016/05/31/world/europe/russia-finland-nato-trolls.html.

Issie Lapowsky, "The State Department's Fumbled Fight Against Russian Propaganda," *Wired*, November 22, 2017, https://www.wired.com/story/the-state-departments-fumbled-fight-against-russian-propaganda/.

Neil MacFarquhar, "Inside the Russian Troll Factory: Zombies and a Breakneck Pace," *New York Times*, February 18, 2018, https://www.nytimes.com/2018/02/18/world/europe/russia-troll-factory.html.

Molly K. McKew, "How Twitter Bots and Trump Fans Made #ReleaseTheMemo Go Viral," *Politico*, February 4, 2018, https://www.politico.com/magazine/story/2018/02/04/trump-twitter-russians-release-the-memo-216935.

George Monbiot, "The need to protect the internet from 'astroturfing' grows ever more urgent," the *Guardian*, February 23, 2011, https://www.theguardian.com/environment/georgemonbiot/2011/feb/23/need-to-protect-internet-from-astroturfing.

George Monbiot, "These astroturf libertarians are the real threat to internet democracy," the *Guardian*, December 13, 2010, https://www.theguardian.com/commentisfree/libertycentral/2010/dec/13/astroturf-libertarians-internet-democracy.

Alicia Parlapiano and Jasmine C. Lee, "The Propaganda Tools Used by Russians to Influence the 2016 Election," *New York Times*, February 16, 2018, https://www.nytimes.com/ interactive/2018/02/16/us/politics/russia-propaganda-election-2016.html.

Matthew Rosenberg, Charlie Savage, and Michael Wines, "Russia Sees Midterm Elections as Chance to Sow Fresh Discord, Intelligence Chiefs Warn," *New York Times*, February 13, 2018, https://www.nytimes.com/2018/02/13/ us/politics/russia-sees-midterm-elections-as-chance-to-sow-fresh-discord-intelligence-chiefs-warn. html?ref=topics.

Max Seddon, "Documents Show How Russia's Troll Army Hit America," *Buzzfeed*, Juen 2, 2014, https://www.buzzfeed. com/maxseddon/documents-show-how-russias-troll-army-hit-america.

Craig Silverman and Lawrence Alexander, "How Teens In The Balkans Are Duping Trump Supporters With Fake News," *Buzzfeed*, November 3, 2016, https://www.buzzfeed.com/ craigsilverman/how-macedonia-became-a-global-hub-for-pro-trump-misinfo.

Claire Wardle and Hossein Derakhshan, "Information Disorder: Toward an interdisciplinary framework for research and policymaking," Council of Europe, September 27, 2017, https://shorensteincenter.org/wp-content/ uploads/2017/10/PREMS-162317-GBR-2018-Report-de%CC%81sinformation.pdf?x78124.

David Wertime, "Meet the Chinese Trolls Pumping Out 488 Million Fake Social Media Posts," *Foreign Policy*, May 19, 2016, http://foreignpolicy.com/2016/05/19/meet-the-chinese-internet-trolls-pumping-488-million-posts-harvard-stanford-ucsd-research/.

Stefan Wojcik, Solomon Messing, Aaron Smith, Lee Rainie, and Paul Hitlin, "Bots in the Twittersphere: An estimated two-thirds of tweeted links to popular websites are posted by automated accounts – not human beings," Pew Research Center, April 9, 2018, http://www.pewinternet. org/2018/04/09/bots-in-the-twittersphere/.

Index